SAVVAS
GRAMMAR PLUS

WORKBOOK

Grade 11

SAVVAS
LEARNING COMPANY

SAVVAS
LEARNING COMPANY

ISBN-13: 978-1-418-38411-1
ISBN-10:   1-418-38411-9

6   23

Contents

iii

MECHANICS

1 NOUNS

A noun is the part of speech that names a person, a place, a thing, or an idea.

There are different types of nouns. See the examples below.

Common Noun	any one of a class of people, places, things, or ideas	sister, state, hour
Proper Noun	specific person, place, thing, or idea (usually capitalized)	Maria, San Francisco, Wednesday
Concrete Noun	something you can see, touch, taste, hear, or smell	couch, pizza, whistling, perfume
Abstract Noun	something you can't perceive through your senses	anger, peace, success

PRACTICE A Identifying Nouns

Read each sentence. Then, underline all the nouns in each sentence.

Example: Her friend was driving that car.
Answer: Her <u>friend</u> was driving that <u>car</u>.

1. The ball is in the grass.
2. Please go to the store for milk.
3. Dinner is in the oven.
4. Call your friend to get the assignment.
5. The weather in Phoenix is hot in July.

6. Jamal went to the library.
7. Your group will make the poster.
8. Success requires hard work.
9. My family visited the beach on Sunday.
10. The dishes are in the cabinet above the sink.

PRACTICE B Labeling Nouns

Read each sentence. Then, on the line provided, identify whether each underlined noun is (1) common *or* proper *and (2)* concrete *or* abstract.

Example: <u>Dad</u> is making <u>dinner</u>.
Answer: <u>Dad</u> — proper, concrete; <u>dinner</u> — common, concrete

1. Your <u>bravery</u> was very impressive. _____
2. <u>Grandpa</u> went to the <u>garage</u>. _____
3. Please finish your <u>homework</u>. _____
4. My <u>cousin</u> lives in <u>Chicago</u>. _____
5. An old <u>house</u> needs a lot of <u>maintenance</u>. _____
6. My <u>bicycle</u> gives me the <u>freedom</u> to explore our <u>neighborhood</u>. _____
7. My <u>belief</u> is that <u>Sam</u> will be fine. _____
8. Have you read *Hamlet* by <u>Shakespeare</u>? _____
9. His <u>understanding</u> grew all <u>week</u>. _____
10. No <u>river</u> is as inspiring as the <u>Mississippi</u>. _____

Writing and Speaking Application

Write a two sentence description of your classroom, using at least six nouns. Circle the nouns. Then, read your sentences to a partner. Your partner should listen for and name the nouns in your sentences. Then, switch roles with your partner.

2 PRONOUNS

A pronoun is a word that stands for a noun or another pronoun.

Pronouns get their meaning from the words they stand for. These words are called the pronouns' *antecedents*. This chart shows several common types of pronouns.

Personal Pronouns	refer to the person speaking, the person spoken to, or the person, place, thing, or idea spoken about	I, me, we, us, you, it, he, him, she, her, they, them
Possessive Pronouns	indicate ownership or possession	my, mine, our, ours, your, yours, its, his, her, hers, their, theirs
Reflexive Pronouns	end in -*self* or -*selves* and indicate that someone or something in the sentence acts for or on itself	myself, ourselves, yourself, yourselves, itself, himself, herself, themselves
Intensive Pronouns	end in -*self* or -*selves* and add emphasis to a noun or pronoun in the sentence	

PRACTICE A Identifying Pronouns and Antecedents

Read each sentence. Then, write the pronoun and its antecedent.

Example: Did Keisha forget her wallet?
Answer: pronoun: her; antecedent: Keisha

1. Issa just completed her first marathon. _____

2. When the car started, it made a rattling sound. _____

3. Ahmed displayed his artwork with pride. _____

4. After Zoe graduated from college, she began law school. _____

5. Nicholas left right after his lesson. _____

6. The plane circled the runway before it landed. _____

PRACTICE B Identifying Possessive, Reflexive, and Intensive Pronouns

Read each sentence. Then, write the pronoun and label it possessive, reflexive, *or* intensive.

Example: After he ate dinner, Demarcus began studying.
Answer: he—personal

1. Lela gave herself a pat on the back.

_____

2. Emily went to her appointment.

_____

3. Felix himself spoke to the group.

_____

4. Madison forgot to charge her phone.

_____

5. Olivia poured herself a glass of juice.

_____

6. Mrs. Ortiz repainted the room herself.

7. Ryan did the laundry himself.

8. The house seems to make its own mess.

9. Elijah always takes his time.

10. Kira and Seth themselves organized the event.

Writing and Speaking Application

Write five sentences that include pronouns. Circle the pronouns and draw arrows to their antecedents. Read your sentences to a partner, who will identify the pronouns and their antecedents. Then, switch roles with your partner.

3 ACTION VERBS AND LINKING VERBS

A verb is a word or a group of words that describes an action, a condition, an occurrence, or a state of being.

There are different types of verbs. See the examples below.

Action Verb	tells what action someone or something is performing	go: goes, is going, went, has gone run: runs, is running, ran, has run fly: flies, is flying, flew, has flown learn: learns, is learning, learned, has learned
Linking Verb	connects a subject with a noun, a pronoun, or an adjective that identifies or describes it	be: am, is, are, is being, was, were, has been feel: feels, is feeling, felt, has felt become: becomes, is becoming, became, has become

PRACTICE A Identifying Action Verbs

Read each sentence. Underline the action verb.

Example: His daughter worries about him.
Answer: His daughter <u>worries</u> about him.

1. Penny writes songs.

2. Jose watches a lot of movies.

3. The family ate at a picnic table.

4. Carla's daughter works as a mechanic.

5. Amir shops for groceries every Wednesday.

PRACTICE B Identifying Linking Verbs

Read each sentence. Underline the linking verb.

Example: Morgan is a kind person.
Answer: Morgan <u>is</u> a kind person.

1. Jin is their youngest child.

2. Matt has become a talented photographer.

3. Your parents seem so proud of you.

4. Kwame feels a little chilly.

5. Sarah looks eager and determined.

PRACTICE C Distinguishing Between Action Verbs and Linking Verbs

Underline the verbs in the following sentences. Then, write whether each verb is an action verb *or a* linking verb.

Example: Isabella felt tired after the long day.
Answer: Isabella <u>felt</u> tired after the long day. <u>linking verb</u>

1. Sofía studied for the math exam. _____

2. Their business won an award. _____

3. Aaron seemed surprised about the result. _____

4. Farah is a published author. _____

5. The basketball team went on a camping trip. _____

Writing and Speaking Application

Write five sentences—some in which you use an action verb and some in which you use a linking verb. Read your sentences to a partner. Your partner should listen for and name each verb and tell whether it is an action verb or a linking verb. Then, switch roles with your partner.

4 TRANSITIVE AND INTRANSITIVE VERBS

A transitive verb is a verb that has a direct object. An intransitive verb is a verb that does *not* have a direct object.

The word that receives the action of a transitive verb is called the *direct object*. You can determine whether a verb has a direct object by asking *Whom?* or *What?* after the verb.

Transitive: The boy lost his jacket. (Lost *what?* his jacket)

Intransitive: The baby cried loudly. (Cried *what?* [no answer])

PRACTICE A Identifying Transitive Verbs and Their Objects

Read each sentence. Then, underline the verb and circle the direct object.

Example: Darnell shoveled snow after the storm.
Answer: Darnell <u>shoveled</u> (snow) after the storm.

1. Kwon saw Tyler at the grocery store.
2. Wendy posted new pictures of her family.
3. Mr. Kim bought a ticket for his daughter.
4. Antonio got a new job.
5. Elise took her medicine on time.

6. Camila rode her skateboard to school.
7. Arjun assisted his grandfather.
8. The icy roads caused accidents.
9. Kody knew the answers to that test.
10. Amanda helped her sister with the chores.

PRACTICE B Distinguishing Between Transitive Verbs and Intransitive Verbs

Read each sentence. Then, write the action verb, and label it transitive *or* intransitive.

Example: Miguel added milk to the cake batter.
Answer: added — transitive

1. Mr. Svita confirmed his son's plans. _____

2. That building towers over all the others. _____

3. Dennis walks for exercise. _____

4. John babysits his cousins after school. _____

5. Alberto admires that musician. _____

6. The weather ruined our plans. _____

7. This computer drive stores several thousand files. _____

8. Taran grew incredibly in one year. _____

9. Her lessons start at nine in the morning. _____

10. The toddler fell while running. _____

Writing and Speaking Application

Write four sentences, two with transitive verbs and two with intransitive verbs. Then, read your sentences to a partner. Your partner should listen for each verb and identify it as *transitive* or *intransitive*. Then, switch roles with your partner.

5 VERB PHRASES

A verb phrase consists of a main verb and one or more helping verbs.

Helping verbs are added before the main verb to form a verb phrase. For example, in the sentence "I will be arriving at school on time," *will* and *be* are helping verbs, and *arriving* is the main verb.

Common helping verbs are shown below.

Forms of *be*	am, is, has been, was being, will be, will have been, should be, had been, might have been
Other Helping Verbs	do, does, did, have, has, had, shall, should, will, would, can, could, may, might, must

PRACTICE A Recognizing Verb Phrases

Read each sentence. Then, write the verb phrase in it.

Example: She is interested in nutrition.
Answer: <u>is interested</u>

1. Beth is blogging about the news. _____
2. His cousin is studying law. _____
3. Karma was living next door. _____
4. The car is running on fumes. _____
5. I am planning for vacation. _____
6. The weather has been getting colder. _____
7. Nestor is talking on the phone. _____
8. Grandma is shopping for new curtains. _____
9. Her mail was piling up. _____
10. Stephanie has been trying to learn Chinese. _____

PRACTICE B Identifying Helping Verbs and Main Verbs

Read each sentence. Circle each main verb, and underline all helping verbs.

Example: I have been wondering about travel.
Answer: I <u>have been</u> (wondering) about travel.

1. Mr. Ruiz is making a documentary.
2. Yusuf is building a bookcase.
3. The newspaper has been reporting on the war.
4. You do like ice cream, right?
5. Terra is going to band practice.
6. Dave has been fostering a dog.
7. Michelle is using common sense.
8. Luis is planning for college.
9. The police were working double shifts.
10. Mr. Nguyen has won awards for his poetry.

Writing and Speaking Application

Write three sentences in which you use verb phrases. Circle the main verbs, and underline the helping verbs. Then, read your sentences to a partner. Your partner should identify which words are main verbs and which words are helping verbs. Switch roles with your partner and repeat the exercise.

6 ADJECTIVES

An adjective is a word used to describe a noun or a pronoun or to give it a more specific meaning.

An adjective answers one of four questions about a noun or a pronoun: *What kind? Which one? How many? How much?* See the examples below. Note that a noun may be used as an adjective, as in the first example.

<u>flower</u> gardens	What kind of gardens? (flower)
<u>that</u> lesson	Which lesson? (that)
<u>sixty-seven</u> years	How many years? (sixty-seven)
<u>boundless</u> energy	How much energy? (boundless)

PRACTICE A Identifying Adjectives

Read the sentences below. Then, underline the adjective or adjectives in each sentence. Remember that articles (a, an, the) *and possessive pronouns (such as* my *and* your) *are adjectives, too!*

Example: Those complicated recipes don't interest me.
Answer: <u>Those complicated</u> recipes don't interest me.

1. Some colds really drag on.
2. Tamara loves old rap music.
3. Noah wore a gray hat.
4. Most Italian food is wonderful.
5. Timothy found an antique coin.
6. That big dog is named Teddy.
7. Susan makes the best apple pie.
8. The poet described a ruined cottage.
9. Medieval architecture fascinates me.
10. Riding my bike is my favorite activity.

PRACTICE B Identifying Nouns Used as Adjectives

Read each sentence. Then, write the noun or nouns used as an adjective.

Example: Emma went to the science lab.
Answer: science

1. The sports car sparkled in the sunshine. _____
2. Jacque skips guitar practice on Wednesdays. _____
3. We used wheat bread to make the sandwiches. _____
4. Dr. Weston is a bone expert. _____
5. The apple juice is in the fridge. _____
6. The gravel road needs work. _____
7. The can label contains nutrition information. _____
8. My grandma uses unscented laundry soap. _____
9. My uncle is a truck driver. _____
10. The governor discussed traffic issues. _____

Writing and Speaking Application

Write a three-sentence description of someone you know, using at least one adjective in every sentence. Circle the adjectives. Then, read your sentences to a partner. Your partner should listen for and name the adjective or adjectives in each sentence. Then, switch roles with your partner.

7 ADVERBS

An adverb is a word that modifies a verb, an adjective, or another adverb.

When an adverb modifies a verb, it will answer one of the following questions: *Where? When? In what way? To what extent?* When an adverb modifies an adjective or another adverb, it will answer the question *To what extent?* See the examples below.

Where?	The book is <u>here</u>.
When?	Jacob <u>never</u> walked the dog.
In what way?	Brianna <u>kindly</u> offered to help.
To what extent?	They <u>completely</u> lost track of time.

PRACTICE A Recognizing Adverbs

Read each sentence. Then, write the adverb in each sentence.

Example: Lucia seldom goes on social media.
Answer: <u>seldom</u>

1. Mrs. Farrar always recycles. _____
2. Joshua accidentally broke the glass. _____
3. Brittany drives carefully. _____
4. We enjoy eating slowly. _____
5. Tashi is learning English quickly. _____

6. The toddler often feels frustrated. _____
7. Jana solved the math problem easily. _____
8. I often donate to the shelter. _____
9. Oscar opened the gift carefully. _____
10. Sam vaguely remembers his childhood. _____

PRACTICE B Identifying Adverbs and the Words They Modify

Read each sentence. Then, write the adverb and the word or words it modifies.

Example: Gophers live underground.
Answer: <u>underground— live</u>

1. Rose smiled gratefully. _____
2. I finally finished the project. _____
3. The sun shines everywhere. _____
4. Mr. Gutiérrez carefully arranged the flowers. _____
5. The weather is especially cold for this time of year. _____
6. Pikes Peak is a really beautiful mountain. _____
7. I try to cure my colds naturally. _____
8. The speaker nervously cleared his throat. _____
9. Aisha responded enthusiastically to the job offer. _____
10. The celebration occurs annually. _____

Writing and Speaking Application

Write a three-sentence description of how to do something, using at least three adverbs. Circle the adverbs. Then, read your sentences to a partner. Your partner should listen for and name the adverbs in your sentences. Then, switch roles with your partner.

8 PREPOSITIONS AND PREPOSITIONAL PHRASES

A preposition relates the noun or pronoun that appears with it to another word in the sentence.

A prepositional phrase is a group of words that includes a preposition and a noun or pronoun, as well as any modifiers.

Prepositions show relationships that involve location, direction, time, cause, or possession. Some prepositions consist of more than one word. Here are some common prepositions:

> *about, above, across, across from, against, along, among, around, at, because of, before, behind, below, beneath, beside, between, by, down, during, for, from, in, in front of, into, near, of, off, on, on top of, onto, over, through, to, toward, under, upon, with, within, without*

Prepositions come at the beginnings of prepositional phrases. A *prepositional phrase* includes a preposition, a noun or pronoun that is called the *object of the preposition*, and any word or words that modify the noun or pronoun.

PRACTICE A Identifying Prepositions and Prepositional Phrases
Read each sentence. Then, write the prepositional phrase and underline the preposition.

Example: The boy sat on his dad's shoulders.
Answer: on his dad's shoulders

1. Put the apples in the refrigerator. _____
2. The top of the car is faded. _____
3. School starts at eight. _____
4. I saw an elk in the mountains. _____
5. He polished the wood with oil. _____
6. Marie used to live in Georgia. _____
7. Your shoes are under your bed. _____
8. Angel dreams about flying. _____
9. He sent a package to his mother. _____
10. Nina left her books on the table. _____

PRACTICE B Identifying Prepositions and Their Objects
Read each sentence. Then, underline the preposition, and circle the object of the preposition.

Example: Penny swam across the lake.
Answer: Penny swam across the (lake.)

1. The movie begins at 9:00 PM.
2. Our dog sat under the table.
3. The air smells fresh after the rain.
4. Jaime strolled toward the beach.
5. The squirrel jumped into the air.

6. The bee buzzed among the flowers.
7. Mateo is the son of a teacher.
8. The bear trampled through the brush.
9. Ang likes extra frosting on his cake.
10. Never ride a bike without a helmet.

Writing and Speaking Application
Write four sentences that include a prepositional phrase in each. Underline the prepositions. Then, read your sentences to a partner. Your partner should listen for and name the prepositional phrases. Together, identify the objects of the prepositions. Then, switch roles with your partner.

9 CONJUNCTIONS

A conjunction is a word used to connect words or groups of words.

There are three main kinds of conjunctions: *coordinating, correlative,* and *subordinating*.

A **coordinating conjunction** joins grammatically equivalent elements, such as two nouns or two independent clauses. There are only seven coordinating conjunctions, listed to the right.	and, but, for, nor, or, so, yet
A **correlative conjunction** is used in pairs and joins grammatically equivalent elements. There are only five pairs of correlative conjunctions, listed to the right.	both…and; either…or; neither…nor; not only…but also; whether…or
A **subordinating conjunction** introduces a dependent, or subordinate, clause. There are many different subordinating conjunctions; this chart shows some of the most common ones.	after, because, before, although, as if, as long as, so that, whenever, when, where, as though, in order that, while

PRACTICE A Identifying Conjunctions

Read the following sentences. Then, underline the conjunctions. If a sentence has a pair of correlative conjunctions, remember to underline both parts.

Example: DeShaun plans to study either math or science.
Answer: DeShaun plans to study <u>either</u> math <u>or</u> science.

1. After you eat dinner, you may have some dessert.

2. We will eat either soup or sandwiches.

3. Before I go to bed, I need to finish my homework.

4. Would you rather rake or mow?

5. After you wash the outside of the car, please vacuum the inside.

6. When I eat heavy food, I feel tired.

7. Both Erin and Shawn are on the tennis team.

8. Dawn can take ballet or tap.

9. Because she wants to stay healthy, my grandmother lifts weights.

10. The driveway gets dangerous when it snows.

PRACTICE B Identifying Types of Conjunctions

Read each sentence below. Then, write the conjunction or pair of conjunctions from each sentence, and label it coordinating, correlative, *or* subordinating.

Example: Although I don't like homework, I love good grades.
Answer: <u>Although—subordinating</u>

1. I need to finish my chores, or I will get grounded. _____

2. Luis is tired but willing to help. _____

3. Whenever we go to the skatepark, we have fun. _____

4. As long as you work hard, you will succeed. _____

5. Taylor will either cook dinner or wash the dishes. _____

6. You must have both tape and glue for this project. _____

Writing and Speaking Application

Write three sentences: one that uses a coordinating conjunction, one that uses a pair of correlative conjunctions, and one that uses a subordinating conjunction. Read your sentences to a partner, who should identify the type of conjunction used in each sentence. Then, switch roles with your partner.

10 INTERJECTIONS

An interjection is a word or group of words that expresses feeling or emotion and functions independently of a sentence.

Interjections are different from most other words because they do not have a grammatical connection to other words in a sentence. Some common interjections are shown in the table below.

ah	dear	hey	oh	well
aha	goodbye	hello	ouch	whew
alas	goodness	hurray	psst	wow

PRACTICE A Identifying Interjections

Underline the interjection in each item below.

Example: Hey! It's great to see you!
Answer: <u>Hey</u>! It's great to see you!

1. Ahem. Can everybody hear me?
2. By the way, I think you look great!
3. Wow! What a great play!
4. Aw, what a cute puppy!
5. Psst, did you hear that last part?

6. Hurray! Lidia and Kyle are here!
7. Ouch! I shut my thumb in the door.
8. Attention! Flight 1016 to Boston has been delayed.
9. Yikes! That's expensive!
10. What? I don't believe that for a minute.

PRACTICE B Supplying Interjections

Circle the interjection that shows the feeling expressed in the sentence.

Example: (Yuck! / Yum!) This is delicious!
Answer: (Yuck! /(Yum!))

1. (Awesome! / Alas,) I finally found my phone!
2. (Whew! / Oh no!) I think I caught a cold.
3. (Yikes! / Great!) That's wonderful news!
4. (Phew! / Oops!) I just spilled my coffee.
5. (Uh-oh, / Hurray,) we forgot to pack the beach towels!
6. (Whoa! / Yippee!) That was a close one!
7. (Argh, / Ahh,) it feels great to finally be on vacation.
8. (Whew, / Meh,) I didn't think the movie was very good.
9. (Ah, / Ahem,) don't worry about it.
10. (Phew! / Oops!) We just made it on time!

Writing and Speaking Application

Write four sentences, each using an interjection that appears on this page. Circle the interjections. Then, read your sentences to a partner. Your partner should listen for and name the interjections. Then, switch roles with your partner.

11 IDENTIFYING PARTS OF SPEECH

The way a word is used in a sentence determines its part of speech.

A word's job (or part of speech) in one sentence can be different from its job (or part of speech) in another sentence. Consider the information in the table below.

Noun	a word that names a person, a place, a thing, or an idea	The <u>boy</u> threw the <u>ball</u>.
Pronoun	a word that stands for a noun or another pronoun	<u>He</u> threw the ball.
Verb	a word showing an action, a condition, or a state of being	The boy <u>threw</u> the ball.
Adjective	a word that modifies (or describes) a noun or a pronoun	The <u>tall</u> boy threw the ball.
Adverb	a word that modifies a verb, an adjective, or another adverb	The boy <u>skillfully</u> threw the ball.
Preposition	a word that relates a noun or pronoun that appears with it to another word	The boy threw the ball <u>toward</u> his dad.
Conjunction	a word that connects words or groups of words	The boy threw the ball, <u>and</u> his dad caught it.
Interjection	a word that expresses emotion	<u>Wow</u>! He threw the ball far!

PRACTICE A Identifying Parts of Speech: Nouns, Pronouns, Verbs, Adjectives, and Adverbs

Read each sentence. Then, identify whether the underlined word is a noun, a pronoun, a verb, an adjective, or an adverb.

Example: She <u>took</u> a walk on her break.

Answer:	She <u>took</u> a walk on her break.	noun	pronoun	(verb)	adjective	adverb
1.	<u>He</u> works hard all day.	noun	pronoun	verb	adjective	adverb
2.	Miette <u>takes</u> singing lessons.	noun	pronoun	verb	adjective	adverb
3.	Connie works in a <u>restaurant</u>.	noun	pronoun	verb	adjective	adverb
4.	Alejandro likes <u>stand-up</u> comedy.	noun	pronoun	verb	adjective	adverb
5.	The moon is shining <u>dimly</u>.	noun	pronoun	verb	adjective	adverb

PRACTICE B Identifying Parts of Speech: Prepositions, Conjunctions, and Interjections

Read each sentence. Then, identify whether the underlined word is a preposition, a conjunction, or an interjection.

Example: The sun moves <u>toward</u> the west.

Answer:	The sun moves <u>toward</u> the west.	(preposition)	conjunction	interjection
1.	Put your homework <u>on</u> my desk.	preposition	conjunction	interjection
2.	<u>Ugh</u>! I think I'm getting a cold.	preposition	conjunction	interjection
3.	We just talked <u>about</u> old times.	preposition	conjunction	interjection
4.	Do you prefer brown <u>or</u> white gravy?	preposition	conjunction	interjection
5.	Meme <u>and</u> Evie are her daughters.	preposition	conjunction	interjection

Writing and Speaking Application

Write four sentences, each including at least one noun, adjective, verb, and adverb. Then, read your sentences to a partner. After reading each sentence, ask your partner to identify each noun, verb, adjective, and adverb. Then, switch roles with your partner.

12 SUBJECTS AND PREDICATES

Every complete sentence has two main parts: a subject and a predicate.

The *complete subject* of a sentence consists of a noun or a pronoun (known as the *simple subject*) plus all of its modifiers. These words tell *whom* or *what* the sentence is about. The *complete predicate* of a sentence consists of a verb or a verb phrase (known as the *simple predicate*) plus all of its objects, complements, and modifiers. These words tell what the subject of the sentence is or does.

The following chart shows the complete subjects and complete predicates of three example sentences. In each example, the simple subject and the simple predicate are underlined.

Complete Subjects	Complete Predicates
The glass of juice	is sitting on the table next to the couch.
The very sick fox	stayed in its den all day.
My geology paper	will be submitted right after class.

PRACTICE A Identifying Simple Subjects

In each sentence below, the complete subject is underlined. Circle the simple subject (which will be part of the underlined section).

Example: The students in the gym began to stretch.
Answer: The (students) in the gym began to stretch.

1. The boy with the green shirt spilled his juice.
2. The kitten in the basket cried for its mother.
3. The books on the top shelf haven't been read.
4. The car needs a tune-up.
5. The bikes in the garage need to be repaired.
6. Roberto's watch sat on the table.
7. The party that we planned never happened.
8. The football players prepared for practice.
9. Their ambitious dream was to be state champions.
10. Their fans knew they could win.

PRACTICE B Identifying Simple Predicates

In each sentence below, the complete predicate is underlined. Circle the simple predicate (which will be part of the underlined section).

Example: Henry lifted the heavy package onto the counter.
Answer: Henry (lifted) the heavy package onto the counter.

1. Romeo's roses will make her smile.
2. The rocky, steep hillside rose above us.
3. Susan prepared dinner for the family last night.
4. The dishes in the sink were washed after supper.
5. Anthony waited before beginning his work.
6. The cheerleader cheered for the excited crowd.
7. Sophia placed all the chairs on the back porch.
8. The chef prepared his various ingredients.
9. The team finished its practice.
10. The turtle retracts its head into its shell.

Writing and Speaking Application

Write four sentences, and underline the simple subject and simple predicate in each. Read your sentences to a partner, who should listen for and name the simple subject and the simple predicate in each sentence. Then, switch roles with your partner.

13 FRAGMENTS

A fragment is a group of words that lacks a subject, a predicate, or both. It does not express a complete unit of thought.

Fragments are not usually used in writing because they might not be understood. Fragments can be corrected by adding the parts that are needed to make a complete thought. See the examples in the table below.

Fragments	Complete Sentences
the frog with warts	The frog with warts plopped into the pond. (added a predicate)
live in those woods	Beautiful elk live in those woods. (added a subject)

PRACTICE A Distinguishing Sentences and Fragments

Each item below is punctuated as if it were a sentence, but some of the items are fragments. Read each item, and write whether it is a sentence *or a* fragment.

Example: The student who loves homework.
Answer: fragment

1. Was starting homework. _____
2. Swimming is fun. _____
3. Easier with practice. _____
4. Eduardo took the test again. _____
5. He hoped for. _____

6. Is an important step. _____
7. I love to celebrate. _____
8. Was difficult to imagine. _____
9. Isaac finished with pride. _____
10. Sonya quickly sat down. _____

PRACTICE B Fixing Fragments

Read each fragment below. Then, use each fragment in a sentence.

Example: on the table
Answer: I left the dishes sitting on the table.

1. the lovable dog _____
2. fell loudly on the floor _____
3. the beautiful view _____
4. sat down on the chair _____
5. jumping over the fence _____
6. the creaky old swing _____
7. his best friend _____
8. the neatest trick _____
9. the computer keyboard _____
10. the first day of school _____

Writing and Speaking Application

Write four fragments and read them to a partner. Together, decide how the fragments can be made into sentences. Then, switch roles with your partner.

14 SUBJECTS IN DECLARATIVE SENTENCES BEGINNING WITH *HERE* OR *THERE*

Here and *there* are never the subject of a sentence.

When the word *here* or *there* begins a declarative sentence, it is usually an adverb that modifies the verb by pointing out where something is located. Usually, a sentence beginning with *here* or *there* is inverted (with the subject following the verb). If you rearrange the sentence in subject-verb order, you can more easily identify the subject of the sentence. In each of the examples shown below, the subject is underlined, and the verb is set in boldface.

Sentences Beginning With *Here* or *There*	Sentences Rearranged in Subject-Verb Order
Here **is** your backpack.	Your backpack **is** here.
There **is** a crack in the foundation.	A crack **is** in the foundation.

PRACTICE A Rearranging Sentences Beginning With *Here* or *There*
Read each sentence below. Then, rearrange it so that it is written in subject-verb order.

Example: There is sugar in the bowl.
Answer: Sugar is in the bowl.

  1. There are clouds in the sky. _____

  2. There is snow on the ground. _____

  3. Here is the calculator for the math test. _____

  4. There are some people talking. _____

  5. There is a sock in the dryer. _____

  6. Here are the answers. _____

  7. Here is the order for your new books. _____

  8. There are coins in the dish. _____

  9. There is a guitar in the case. _____

10. Here is an apple pie. _____

PRACTICE B Identifying Subjects and Verbs in Sentences Beginning With *Here* or *There*
Read each sentence. Then, underline the subject and circle the verb.

Example: There is a knot in the rope.
Answer: There (is) a knot in the rope.

  1. There is a car in the garage.
  2. There are many trees in my yard.
  3. Here is your package.
  4. There is a glass in the cabinet.
  5. There are excuses for your absence.

  6. Here is your backpack.
  7. There are some people in the pool.
  8. Here is the material for your project.
  9. There are several pots on the stove.
10. Here is your football.

Writing and Speaking Application
Write four sentences that begin with *here* or *there*. Underline the subjects and circle the verbs. Then, read your sentences to a partner. Your partner should identify the subject and verb of each sentence. Then, switch roles with your partner.

15 SUBJECTS IN INTERROGATIVE SENTENCES

In an interrogative sentence, the subject often follows the verb.

Interrogative sentences are questions. Some interrogative sentences use subject-verb order, but usually they are inverted (verb-subject). To help locate the subject, rearrange interrogative sentences into subject-verb order. Consider the examples in the table below, which show the subject underlined and the verb(s) in boldface.

Interrogative Sentences	Rearranged in Subject-Verb Order
Is the library open on Sunday?	The library **is** open on Sunday?
Did you **borrow** my book?	You **did borrow** my book?
Where **is** the party?	The party **is** where?

PRACTICE A Rearranging Interrogative Sentences

Read each sentence below. Then, rearrange each sentence so that it is written in subject-verb order.

Example: Where is the museum?
Answer: The museum is where?

1. What are you thinking? _____
2. Where is the party? _____
3. Are you feeling upset? _____
4. What is the solution to this problem? _____
5. Are they expecting us this evening? _____
6. Why are sunsets better in Florida? _____
7. Are you going to the beach with your family? _____
8. When should I put the casserole in the oven? _____
9. How did you manage that job? _____
10. Why are you feeling grouchy? _____

PRACTICE B Identifying Subjects and Verbs in Interrogative Sentences

Read each sentence. Then, circle the subject of the sentence and underline the verb(s). Some of the sentences have both a main verb and a helping verb.

Example: Why are you whispering?
Answer: Why are(you)whispering?

1. Why did your mom say no?
2. How can I change your mind?
3. Why do you like that swimming pool?
4. Why did Lee call his uncle?
5. Where is your dad?

6. Are you buying new shoes?
7. Why is Zoe leaving early?
8. Will your brother be at the party?
9. What do you think?
10. How is Anita's friend feeling now?

Writing and Speaking Application

Write four interrogative sentences (questions). Circle the subject of each and underline the verb(s). Next, read your sentences to a partner, who will listen for and name the subject and verb(s) in each sentence. Finally, switch roles with your partner.

Name _____ Date _____

16 SUBJECTS IN IMPERATIVE SENTENCES

In an imperative sentence, the subject is understood to be *you*.

The subject of an imperative sentence is usually implied instead of being specifically stated. Consider the examples in the table below.

Imperative Sentences	Sentences With *You* Added
First, do your homework.	First, [you] do your homework.
After school, come directly home.	After school, [you] come directly home.
Clean the kitchen, please.	[You] clean the kitchen, please.

PRACTICE A Rewriting Imperative Sentences to Include *You*

Read each sentence below. Then, rewrite it to include its subject, you.

Example: Take a nap after lunch.
Answer: You take a nap after lunch.

1. Later, watch a movie. _____
2. Relax on the sofa. _____
3. By tomorrow, finish all your work. _____
4. Make the bed after you get up. _____
5. Watch the children. _____
6. Paint the picture with watercolors. _____
7. Finish the game, please. _____
8. Decide which book to read. _____
9. Feed the cat. _____
10. Tell me later. _____

PRACTICE B Writing Imperative Sentences

On the lines below, write imperative sentences that have the implied subject you.

Example: Always wear a seatbelt when you are driving.

1. _____
2. _____
3. _____
4. _____
5. _____

Writing and Speaking Application

Write four imperative sentences and read them to a partner. Your partner should restate each sentence to include the subject, *you*. Then, switch roles with your partner.

17 SUBJECTS IN EXCLAMATORY SENTENCES

In an exclamatory sentence, part of the complete predicate comes before the subject and the verb.

The term *exclamation* is often used to describe any sentence that expresses strong emotion and ends with an exclamation point. However, a true *exclamatory* (or *exclamative*) *sentence* is one that begins with *What* or *How* and has a particular form: Part of the complete predicate, such as the direct object or the subject complement, comes before the subject and the verb.

To locate the subject of an exclamatory sentence, rearrange the sentence in subject-predicate order. Either omit the word *how* or *what*, or try replacing it with the word *so* or *such*. Consider the examples in this chart, in which the subjects are underlined and the verbs appear in boldface.

Form	Example	Rearranged in Subject-Predicate Order
Begins With *How*	How beautiful your <u>eyes</u> **are**!	Your <u>eyes</u> **are** [so] beautiful!
Begins With *What*	What beautiful eyes <u>you</u> **have**!	<u>You</u> **have** [such] beautiful eyes!

PRACTICE A Identifying Subjects and Verbs in Exclamatory Sentences

Read each sentence below. Underline the subject of each sentence, and circle the verb or verb phrase.

Example: What an exciting trip you had!

Answer: What an exciting trip <u>you</u> (had!)

1. How masterfully that violinist plays!

2. What a moving speech the veteran delivered!

3. How devious your plan sounds!

4. What a lifelike portrait you have drawn!

5. How ominuosly those clouds gather!

6. What a delightful meal we just shared!

PRACTICE B Writing Exclamatory Sentences

On each line below, write an exclamatory sentence. Underline the subject of each sentence, and circle the verb.

Example: How hilarious that <u>movie</u> (was!)

1. _____

2. _____

3. _____

4. _____

5. _____

Writing and Speaking Application

Write four exclamatory sentences, and read them to a partner. Your partner should identify the subject and the verb in each sentence. Then, switch roles with your partner.

18 DIRECT OBJECTS

A direct object is a noun, a pronoun, or a group of words acting as a noun that receives the action of a transitive verb.

Direct objects complete the meaning of action verbs by telling *who* or *what* receives the action. Verbs that have direct objects are called **transitive verbs;** they *transfer* their action onto direct objects. Some verbs are **intransitive**, meaning nothing receives the action of the verb, and the questions *Who(m)?* and *What?* cannot be answered.

Sentence	Question to Ask	Direct Object? Transitive or Intransitive?
She makes cookies for her friends.	She makes *whom* or *what*?	cookies; *transitive*
Fish can breathe through their gills.	Fish can breathe *whom* or *what*?	[no answer]; *intransitive*
Sam hugged his mother.	Sam hugged *whom* or *what*?	mother; *transitive*

PRACTICE A Identifying Direct Objects

The sentences below have transitive verbs, so each verb has a direct object. Read each sentence and underline its direct object.

Example: Susan asked a question.
Answer: Susan asked a question.

1. Sam burnt the toast.
2. Joseph needs a notebook.
3. The boys played baseball.
4. The teacher graded our homework.
5. He removed the pictures from the wall.

6. The children played games at the party.
7. I have a minute.
8. Did you take your vitamins?
9. The pilot flew the airplane.
10. The wrestler is lifting weights.

PRACTICE B Identifying Sentences With Direct Objects

Read each sentence below. Then, on the line provided, write Yes *if the sentence has a direct object, or write* No *if it does not have a direct object.*

Example: Diego painted many murals.
Answer: Diego painted many murals. Yes

1. Jacob worries too much. _____
2. I sank the boat in the river. _____
3. Rainbows thrill Santiago. _____
4. Josie craves frozen yogurt. _____
5. Martina's school just opened. _____
6. The jury finally arrived. _____

Writing and Speaking Application

Write three sentences that have direct objects and three that do not. Read your sentences to a partner. Your partner should say *yes* if a sentence has a direct object or say *no* if it does not. Then, switch roles with your partner.

Name _____ Date _____

19 INDIRECT OBJECTS

An indirect object is a noun or a pronoun that appears with a direct object and tells *to whom, to what, for whom,* or *for what* a transitive verb's action is done.

Only sentences with direct objects can have indirect objects. To locate an indirect object, ask questions such as those shown in the table below. Notice that the second example does not have a direct object, so it cannot have an indirect object.

Sentence	Question to Ask	Direct or Indirect Object
Juan reads his sister a story.	1. Reads *whom* or *what*?	story (direct object)
	2. Reads a story *to whom, to what, for whom,* or *for what?*	sister (indirect object)
She works quickly.	1. Works *whom* or *what*?	[no answer; no direct or indirect object]
Mia gave her mom a kiss on the cheek.	1. Gave *whom* or *what*?	kiss (direct object)
	2. Gave a kiss *to whom, to what, for whom,* or *for what?*	mom (indirect object)

PRACTICE A Identifying Direct Objects and Indirect Objects

Read each sentence below. Then, underline the direct object, and circle the indirect object. Use the chart above to help you ask the necessary questions.

Example: He gave his dad a hug.
Answer: He gave his (dad) a hug.

1. He gave his friend some documents.
2. Carlos brought his brother an apple.
3. Jennifer gave her husband a gift.
4. I asked my partner a question.
5. They saved their friend a seat.
6. Emily served her mother dinner.
7. Melinda showed her husband a picture.
8. She sent the president a letter.
9. They bought their team a new ball.
10. The banker handed me a check.

PRACTICE B Identifying Sentences With Indirect Objects

Read each sentence below. If a sentence does not have an indirect object, write No on the line next to it. If a sentence does have an indirect object, write Yes.

Example: Koto served his wife breakfast.
Answer: Koto served his wife breakfast. Yes

1. Ms. Velasquez served Adam some punch. _____
2. I asked the manager a question. _____
3. Cynthia gave me an award. _____
4. The boys discovered a hidden treasure. _____
5. Bill's dad ate the pizza. _____
6. Poncho showed his friend a painting _____
7. Maria gave me some advice. _____
8. Mr. Kim gave a final speech. _____

Writing and Speaking Application

Write three sentences that have indirect objects. Read your sentences to a partner. Your partner should identify the indirect object in each sentence. Then, switch roles with your partner.

Name _____ Date _____

20 OBJECT COMPLEMENTS

An object complement is an adjective or a noun that appears with a direct object and describes or renames it.

An object complement almost always follows a direct object. Object complements occur only with such verbs as *appoint, call, consider, declare, deem, elect, find, judge, label, make, name, select,* and *think.* The words *to be* (or forms of the verb *to be*) are often understood before an object complement.

The <u>parents</u> <u>found</u> the <u>performance</u> [to be] <u>enchanting</u>.
    subject   verb   direct object   object complement

PRACTICE A Identifying Object Complements

Read each sentence. Then, underline its object complement.

Example: The conductor appointed Karl leader of the orchestra.
Answer: The conductor appointed Karl <u>leader</u> of the orchestra.

1. Greg declared the grade outstanding.
2. The club thought its leader remarkable.
3. The principal considered the teacher fabulous.
4. My mother calls me a peacemaker.
5. The people elected Mrs. Chang mayor.
6. Carol considers her grandchild a joy.
7. The peppermint tea made my throat better.
8. Diego declared my work flawless.
9. Justin thought the suggestion helpful.
10. The patient considers the treatment a miracle.

PRACTICE B Completing Sentences With Object Complements

Read each sentence below. Then, fill in the blank with an object complement.

Example: The captain judged the ship _____.
Answer: The captain judged the ship <u>seaworthy.</u>

1. We thought the movie _____.
2. The official judged the play _____.
3. Wilma thought the child _____.
4. The students elected Rosa _____.
5. Mr. Kwan thought the book _____.
6. My father called my car _____.
7. The professor declared the performance _____.
8. Lea thought the building _____.
9. They found the views _____.
10. Grandpa called my gift _____.

Writing and Speaking Application

Write five sentences that have object complements. Read your sentences to a partner. Your partner should identify the object complement in each sentence. Then, switch roles with your partner.

21 SUBJECT COMPLEMENTS

A subject complement is a noun, a pronoun, or an adjective that appears after a linking verb and gives more information about the subject. There are two kinds of subject complements:

A **predicate nominative** is a noun or a pronoun that appears after a linking verb and names or identifies the subject of the sentence: *Joseph is a programmer.*

A **predicate adjective** is an adjective that appears after a linking verb and describes the subject of the sentence: *The weather is* <u>warm</u>.

Some sentences contain compound subject complements: *Joseph is a* <u>programmer</u> *and a* <u>father</u>.

PRACTICE A Identifying Subject Complements

Read each sentence. Then, underline the subject complement or complements in each sentence.

Example: Your sister is sweet and kind.
Answer: Your sister is <u>sweet</u> and <u>kind</u>.

1. Emily seems brilliant.
2. Cathy is a grandmother.
3. Her sister is leader of the band.
4. The highway is dry and safe.
5. The boy's hair looks great.

6. My brother is a dentist.
7. That dessert was decadent.
8. Santiago is a volunteer.
9. The weather report is frightening.
10. The ceiling is white.

PRACTICE B Identifying Predicate Nominatives and Predicate Adjectives

Read each sentence. Then, underline each subject complement. On the line provided, write whether each subject complement is a predicate nominative or a predicate adjective.

Example: My mom is an architect.
Answer: My mom is an <u>architect</u>. predicate nominative

1. She is a professional dancer. _____
2. Julian is funny and smart. _____
3. His suit looks stylish. _____
4. Aya is a lawyer. _____
5. My sister is the state gymnastics champion. _____
6. Desert nights are cold. _____
7. The painting is enormous. _____
8. Mrs. Ramirez is a veteran. _____
9. The pizza is hot and delicious. _____
10. Michelle's daughter is a student. _____

Writing and Speaking Application

Write three sentences that have subject complements. After you read each sentence to a partner, your partner should identify the subject complement and say whether it is a predicate adjective or a predicate nominative. Then, switch roles with your partner.

22 PREPOSITIONAL PHRASES

A prepositional phrase (such as *behind the house*) includes a preposition, a noun or a pronoun (called the object of the preposition), and any word or words that modify the noun or pronoun.

Prepositional phrases can act as adjectives (in which case they are called **adjectival phrases**), or they can act as adverbs (in which case they are called **adverbial phrases**).

Prepositional Phrase Type	Function	Answers the Question	Example
Adjectival Phrase	modifies a noun or a pronoun	*What kind?* or *Which one?*	The man in the red coat held the door open. (*Which* man?)
Adverbial Phrase	modifies a verb, an adjective, or an adverb	*Where? Why? When? In what way?* or *To what extent?*	The cat hid under the bed. (Hid *where?*)

PRACTICE A Identifying Prepositional Phrases

Read each sentence below. Then, underline the prepositional phrase.

Example: John bounced on the trampoline.
Answer: John bounced <u>on the trampoline</u>.

1. They raced through the house.

2. Martina needs time for reflection.

3. We built a fire at the campground.

4. Mindy put her backpack in the car.

5. Sierra made popcorn in the microwave.

6. George delivered pizzas around town.

7. Melissa answers phone calls at her office.

8. Jessie sent a letter to her friend.

9. The kids swim at the beach.

10. Kahlil did skateboard tricks at the park.

PRACTICE B Identifying Adjectival and Adverbial Phrases

Read each sentence below. Then, indicate whether the underlined prepositional phrase is an adjectival phrase or an adverbial phrase by circling the correct answer.

Example: I paddled <u>down the river</u>.

Answer: I paddled <u>down the river</u>.	Adjectival phrase	(Adverbial phrase)
1. I need a case <u>for my guitar</u>.	Adjectival phrase	Adverbial phrase
2. Dad served dessert <u>after family dinner</u>.	Adjectival phrase	Adverbial phrase
3. Brandon practiced <u>before the big game</u>.	Adjectival phrase	Adverbial phrase
4. Mom adopted the puppy <u>with floppy ears</u>.	Adjectival phrase	Adverbial phrase
5. We watched a movie <u>about space flight</u>.	Adjectival phrase	Adverbial phrase

Writing and Speaking Application

Write five sentences that include prepositional phrases. Then, read your sentences to a partner, who should identify the prepositional phrases. Together, decide whether each prepositional phrase is an adjectival phrase or an adverbial phrase. Then, switch roles.

23 APPOSITIVES AND APPOSITIVE PHRASES

An appositive is a noun or a pronoun that appears next to another noun or pronoun and identifies, renames, or explains it. An appositive phrase consists of an appositive plus all of its modifiers.

- An appositive or an appositive phrase usually comes right after the word it modifies.

- When an appositive or an appositive phrase is **nonessential**, or can be removed without altering the basic meaning of the sentence, it is set off with commas. When an appositive or an appositive phrase is **essential** to the meaning of the sentence, commas are not used.

- An appositive or an appositive phrase is a great way to combine two short, choppy sentences into one more-effective sentence. In the example below, two sentences are combined into one sentence that includes an appositive phrase (underlined).

    Original: Sue's car is an old station wagon. Sue's car cannot handle icy roads.
    Revised: Sue's car, <u>an old station wagon</u>, cannot handle icy roads.

PRACTICE A Identifying Appositive Phrases

Read the following sentences. Then, underline the appositive phrase in each sentence.

Example: Jason, the fastest runner, got sick before the meet.
Answer: Jason, <u>the fastest runner</u>, got sick before the meet.

1. Ella, the most experienced engineer, was chosen to lead the project.
2. Tomorrow, the first Monday of the month, is the last day to enroll.
3. Sarah, my cousin from Denver, plays in a band.
4. My decision, a tough choice to make, was to quit the team.
5. Owen, a talented chef, changed the menu.
6. Rowing, a grueling sport, is easy for Rachel.
7. The hikers, a group of virtual strangers, pushed toward the summit.
8. Marco, a longtime volunteer, liked to help people.
9. Miguel's dog, a collie named Sparta, played in the yard.
10. Bill, a very funny guy, kept us laughing the whole time.

PRACTICE B Combining Sentences Using Appositives and Appositive Phrases

Read the pairs of sentences below. Then, combine the two short, choppy sentences into one more-effective sentence by using an appositive or an appositive phrase.

Example: My team needs more practice. My team is called the Mustangs.
Answer: <u>My team, the Mustangs, needs more practice.</u>

1. That snake is a python. That snake crawled under a rock. _____

2. The store by my house is open. The store is called the Veggie Market. _____

3. My sister is a lifeguard. My sister saved a boy's life. _____

4. Maria loves drawing. Maria is John's best friend. _____

Writing and Speaking Application

Write three sentences that have appositives or appositive phrases. Then, read your sentences to a partner. Your partner should listen for and identify the appositive or appositive phrase in each sentence. Then, switch roles with your partner.

24 VERBALS AND VERBAL PHRASES

A verbal is a word that is formed from a verb but that acts as a different part of speech (a noun, an adjective, or an adverb). A verbal phrase consists of a verbal plus all of its modifiers, objects, or complements.

- Three types of verbals (all of which can form verbal phrases) are *participles*, *gerunds*, and *infinitives*. This lesson focuses on participles and participle phrases.

- A **participle** is a type of verbal that acts as an adjective, modifying a noun or a pronoun. The **present participle** of a verb (such as *walking* or *having*) always ends in *-ing*. The **past participle of a regular verb** (such as *defeated*) always ends in *-ed*; the **past participle of an irregular verb** (such as *burnt, written,* or *done*) often ends *in -d, -t, -n, -en,* or *-ne.*

- A **participial phrase** (which also acts as an adjective) consists of a participle plus all of its modifiers, objects, or complements. In each of the following examples, the participle appears in boldface, the participial phrase is underlined, and the phrase's function is indicated in parentheses:
  *He was baffled by the <u>extremely **confusing**</u> rules.* (modifies the noun *rules*)
  *<u>**Written** many years ago</u>, they no longer seemed relevant.* (modifies the pronoun *they*)

PRACTICE A Identifying Participial Phrases

Read each sentence. Then, underline the participial phrase.

Example: Pierre, relieved by his grade, walked home with a smile.
Answer: Pierre, <u>relieved by his grade</u>, walked home with a smile.

1. Energized by the warm weather, the children ran to the park.

2. Gifts created by hand are often the most thoughtful.

3. Our newly arrived guests rang the front doorbell.

4. That painting, made by my friend Steven, is my favorite.

5. The students, tired from their work, asked for a break.

6. Walking through the house at night, I stubbed my toe.

PRACTICE B Distinguishing Participles and Verbs

Read each sentence below. On the line provided, indicate whether the underlined word or words are (1) a verb *(expressing the main action in a clause) or (2) a* participial phrase *(acting as an adjective).*

Example: The postal employee <u>delivered</u> my mail.   **Answer:** <u>verb</u>

1. <u>Heated by coal</u>, the house was cozy all winter. _____

2. The food, <u>left on the counter</u>, was too cold to eat. _____

3. The flowers <u>thrilled</u> Diana. _____

4. <u>Staring at the pizza</u>, Dad was hoping to eat soon. _____

Writing and Speaking Application

Write three sentences that have participial phrases (verbal phrases that describe nouns). Then, read your sentences to a partner. Your partner should listen for and identify the participial phrase in each sentence. Then, switch roles with your partner.

25 INDEPENDENT AND SUBORDINATE CLAUSES

A clause is a group of words that contains a subject and a verb.

- An **independent clause** (also called a *main clause*) can stand by itself as a complete sentence. Every sentence must contain at least one independent clause.

- A **subordinate clause** (also called a *dependent clause*) has a subject and a verb, but it cannot stand alone as a complete sentence.

<u>Owen is new to running</u>, but <u>he hopes to run a marathon someday.</u>
     independent clause   independent clause

<u>Although Owen is new to running</u>, <u>he hopes to run a marathon someday.</u>
     subordinate clause   independent clause

PRACTICE A Distinguishing Independent and Subordinate Clauses

Read each sentence. Then, circle either independent *or* subordinate, *depending upon whether the underlined section is an independent clause or a subordinate clause.*

Example: Dad said I could go <u>if I checked with Mom first</u>.
Answer: Dad said I could go <u>if I checked with Mom first</u>.   independent   (subordinate)

1. Miguel loves the computer <u>that he's seen on TV</u>.   independent   subordinate

2. I like texting, but <u>I'm trying to cut back</u>.   independent   subordinate

3. My sister, <u>who loves traveling</u>, is flying to Greece.   independent   subordinate

4. <u>After the water begins to boil</u>, add the pasta.   independent   subordinate

5. Devon is social, <u>while Mia is more private</u>.   independent   subordinate

6. <u>That car is fast</u>, and it handles well.   independent   subordinate

PRACTICE B Combining Sentences Using Independent and Subordinate Clauses

Read each sentence pair below. On the line provided, combine the two sentences to form one sentence. For two of your sentences, make one clause subordinate (as shown in Example 1). For the other two sentences, let both clauses remain independent (as shown in Example 2).

Example 1: He doesn't like homework. He does it every night.
Answer: <u>Although he doesn't like homework, he does it every night.</u>

Example 2: Jeanie was in a hurry. She didn't make mistakes.
Answer: <u>Jeanie was in a hurry, but she didn't make mistakes.</u>

1. The car was in bad shape. The car made the trip. _____

2. The cake was delicious. It was made from scratch. _____

3. Tommy was tired. He went to school. _____

4. The sun was very bright. I wore sunglasses. _____

Writing and Speaking Application

Write three sentences that have both an independent clause and a subordinate clause. Then, read your sentences to a partner. Your partner should listen for and identify the independent clause and the subordinate clause in each sentence. Then, switch roles with your partner.

26 ADJECTIVAL CLAUSES

An adjectival clause is a type of subordinate clause that acts as an adjective. It modifies a noun or a pronoun in another clause by telling *what kind* or *which one*.

- An **adjectival clause** (also called a *relative clause*) cannot stand alone—in other words, it is a type of subordinate clause that must be connected to an independent clause.

- An adjectival clause usually begins with a **relative pronoun** (such as *who, whom, whose, which,* or *that*). It may also begin with a **relative adverb** (such as *when* or *where*).

Example: The car <u>that had been ticketed</u> was towed away. (The underlined adjectival clause answers the question *Which one?*)

PRACTICE A Identifying Adjectival Clauses

Read the following sentences. Then, underline the adjectival clause in each sentence.

Example: My tool set, which I've had for years, was a gift from my parents.
Answer: My tool set, <u>which I've had for years</u>, was a gift from my parents.

1. The hat that you left outside is ruined.

2. The new student, whom we'd been waiting to meet, finally arrived.

3. The teacher whom they all loved dearly was preparing to retire.

4. I gave Ethan my old bike, which I never used.

PRACTICE B Writing Sentences With Adjectival Clauses

Read the sentences below. Rewrite each sentence by correctly placing the adjectival clause, which appears in parentheses.

Example: The pencil had no lead. (that Jerrod bought)
Answer: <u>The pencil that Jerrod bought had no lead.</u>

1. The TV is huge. (that we bought yesterday)

   _____

2. Maria fell. (who had been mountain biking on a challenging trail)

   _____

3. Zoe solved a math problem. (that was complex and difficult)

   _____

4. Samuel arrived home covered in mud. (who is a farmer)

   _____

Writing and Speaking Application

Write three sentences that include adjectival clauses. Then, read your sentences to a partner. Your partner should listen for and identify each adjectival clause. Then, switch roles with your partner.

27 RESTRICTIVE VS. NONRESTRICTIVE ADJECTIVAL CLAUSES

An adjectival clause may be either restrictive or nonrestrictive.

- A **restrictive** (or **essential**) **adjectival clause** contains information that is essential to the meaning of the sentence. Removing it would create ambiguity, cause confusion, or change the sentence's meaning. A restrictive adjectival clause should *not* be set off with a comma or commas.

  EXAMPLE: The most famous poet <u>who spent her life in Amherst</u> is Emily Dickinson.
  (The underlined adjectival clause is essential to the sentence's meaning, so it is not set off with commas. If the clause were removed, the sentence "The most famous poet … is Emily Dickinson" would have a different meaning and might not necessarily be true.)

- A **nonrestrictive** (or **nonessential**) **adjectival clause** contains information that is not essential to the meaning of the sentence. Removing it from the sentence would not fundamentally alter the sentence's meaning. A nonrestrictive adjectival clause *should* be set off with a comma or commas.

  EXAMPLE: Emily Dickinson, <u>who spent her life in Amherst</u>, is beloved for her poetry.
  (The underlined adjectival clause provides useful information, but removing it would not fundamentally alter the sentence's meaning, so it should be set off with commas.)

- The relative pronouns *who*, *whom*, and *whose* can be used to introduce both types of adjectival clauses. In general, *that* should be used to introduce a restrictive adjectival clause, whereas *which* should be used to introduce a nonrestrictive adjectival clause.

PRACTICE A Distinguishing Restrictive and Nonrestrictive Adjectival Clauses

Read each sentence. Underline the adjectival clause in the sentence. Then, on the line provided, write whether the adjectival clause is restrictive *or* nonrestrictive.

Example: The team that won the championship is from Center City.
Answer: The team <u>that won the championship</u> is from Center City. <u>restrictive</u>

1. My phone, which needs a new battery, is going to die. _____

2. Lucia, who is a full-time student and has a job, is always busy. _____

3. The man who is standing in the checkout line is my math teacher. _____

4. The team that lost is from Miami. _____

PRACTICE B Writing and Punctuating Adjectival Clauses

Read each pair of sentences. On the line provided, combine the sentences into one sentence by using an adjectival clause. Include commas only when appropriate.

Example: I bite my nails. My nails are very short.
Answer: <u>I bite my nails, which are very short.</u>

1. That man is a salesman. That man is friendly. _____

2. You told the joke this morning. The joke was your funniest yet.

   _____

3. This assignment is very difficult. This assignment counts for half of our grade.

   _____

4. Rae is a lawyer. Rae has a young daughter. _____

Writing and Speaking Application

Write three sentences that have adjectival clauses, and read them to a partner. Your partner should identify each adjectival clause and say whether it is restrictive or nonrestrictive. Then, switch roles.

Name _____ Date _____

28 ADVERBIAL CLAUSES

An adverbial clause is a subordinate clause that acts as an adverb. It modifies a verb, an adjective, or an adverb in another clause by telling *where, when, in what way, to what extent, under what condition,* or *why.*

An adverbial clause begins with a subordinating conjunction and contains a subject and a verb. This chart shows some common subordinating conjunctions. Note that some subordinating conjunctions consist of more than one word.

after	as long as	if	though	whenever
although	because	since	unless	where
as	before	so that	until	wherever
as if	even though	than	when	while

Like adjectival clauses, adverbial clauses can be used to combine the information from two sentences into one sentence that shows the relationship between the ideas. In the example below, the adverbial clause is underlined.

Example: You are going out for groceries. You should also pick up the dry cleaning.
As long as you are going out for groceries, you should also pick up the dry cleaning.

PRACTICE A Identifying How Adverbial Clauses Function

Read each sentence. Then, circle the verb or verb phrase that is modified by the underlined adverbial clause.

Example: Whenever I think of you, I smile.
Answer: Whenever I think of you, I (smile.)

1. I will go when I finish my homework.

2. As long as you work hard, you will earn a passing grade.

3. When you finish your painting, I would love to see it.

4. Kiera fixed the car even though she was busy that day.

5. Whenever I'm bored, I read.

6. I slept late because I needed the rest.

PRACTICE B Combining Sentences Using Adverbial Clauses

Read the sentences below. Then, combine each pair of sentences into one sentence by using the subordinating conjunction in parentheses.

Example: You want to reach your full potential. Do your best work. (if)
Answer: If you want to reach your full potential, do your best work.

1. You may have dessert. You eat your dinner. (after)

_____

2. You've done a good job. You will be rewarded. (Since)

_____

3. You were sleeping. Mrs. Ramirez called. (while)

_____

4. I run fast. My cheeks turn red. (when)

_____

Writing and Speaking Application

Write three sentences that have adverbial clauses. Then, read your sentences to a partner. Your partner should listen for and identify the adverbial clause in each sentence. Then, switch roles with your partner.

29 NOUN CLAUSES

A noun clause is a subordinate clause that acts as a noun. In a sentence, a noun clause may act as a subject, a direct object, a predicate nominative, an object of a preposition, or an appositive.

Sometimes, noun clauses can be difficult to identify because they begin with the same introductory words that can be used to begin other types of clauses and phrases (words such as *that, which, who, whom, whose, how, if, what, whatever, where, when, whether,* and *why*). You can test whether a clause is a noun clause by replacing the clause with *it, that thing,* or *that person.* If the sentence still sounds correct, you probably replaced a noun clause.

Notice that the underlined clause in the example below is a noun clause that is acting as the subject of the sentence. You can replace the clause with *it,* and the sentence still sounds correct.

Example: <u>Whatever Bailey does</u> makes me laugh.

PRACTICE A Identifying Noun Clauses

Read the following sentences. Then, underline the noun clause in each sentence.

Example: She told me that I was funny.
Answer: She told me <u>that I was funny</u>.

1. What I had for breakfast tasted great.

2. The best plan, that we stick together, was completely ignored.

3. Whoever thought of this idea must be a genius.

4. I couldn't believe what she was saying.

5. Why you want to hike in the cold is beyond me.

6. Mira explained why she made her decision.

7. She told me which one she wanted.

8. I'll pick whoever is best qualified.

9. I don't understand why the earth spins.

10. I finally understood that Oscar needed my help.

PRACTICE B Distinguishing Adjectival Clauses and Noun Clauses

Some of the clauses underlined below are adjectival clauses (they describe a noun). Others are noun clauses (they take the place of a noun). Read each sentence. Then, write whether the underlined clause is a noun clause or an adjectival clause.

Example: I wanted the bike <u>that had purple fenders</u>.
Answer: <u>adjectival clause</u>

1. <u>Whatever you need</u> will be given to you. _____

2. My greatest wish, <u>which I now realize was foolish</u>, was to leave my hometown. _____

3. She needed the book <u>that I gave her</u>. _____

4. <u>That you truly care about him</u> is obvious to me. _____

5. Tell me <u>what you want to eat</u>, and I will order it for you. _____

Writing and Speaking Application

Write three sentences that have noun clauses. Then, read your sentences to a partner. Your partner should listen for and identify the noun clause in each sentence. Then, switch roles with your partner.

30 THE FOUR STRUCTURES OF SENTENCES

A sentence's structure is determined by the number of independent (or main) clauses and the number of subordinate (or dependent) clauses the sentence contains. The four possible sentence structures are simple, compound, complex, and compound-complex.

This chart shows definitions and examples of the four possible sentence structures:

Sentence Type	Definition	Example
Simple	a single independent clause	Carrie wants chicken for dinner.
Compound	two or more independent clauses	Carrie wants chicken for dinner, but Chris wants fish.
Complex	one independent clause and one or more subordinate clauses	Although Carrie wants chicken for dinner, Chris wants fish.
Compound-Complex	two or more independent clauses and one or more subordinate clauses	Although Chris wants fish for dinner, Carrie wants chicken, so they are going to a restaurant.

PRACTICE A Distinguishing Between Simple and Compound Sentences

Read the following sentences. Then, label each sentence simple *or* compound.

Example: I wanted to finish the game, but my thigh was cramping.
Answer: compound

1. Have you finished your homework? _____

2. We learned about volcanoes in science class. _____

3. Juan enjoys reading, but his brother prefers pottery. _____

4. I know the woman in the green jacket. _____

5. Ellie expressed her opinion, but Olivia disagreed. _____

6. Mom's happiness is important to all of us. _____

7. I would like to work out or to leave now. _____

8. Either you can give up or you can start over. _____

PRACTICE B Identifying the Four Structures of Sentences

Read the sentences below. Then, circle the structure of each sentence from the choices provided.

Example: She asked the question that we all wanted answered.
Answer: She asked the question that we all wanted answered.   compound   (complex)

1. If we hold a fundraiser, we can raise money for the shelter.   simple   complex

2. Although we left early, there was lots of holiday traffic.   complex   compound

3. Normally, I walk to school, but I decided to take the bus because it was raining.   compound-complex   compound

4. Either choice will be a good one.   compound   simple

5. While I cooked, my brother set the table.   simple   complex

Writing and Speaking Application

Write three sentences, and identify which structure is used in each. Then, read your sentences to a partner. Your partner should listen for and identify the structure of each sentence. Then, switch roles with your partner.

31 THE FOUR FUNCTIONS OF SENTENCES

Sentences can be classified according to how they function—that is, whether they state ideas, ask questions, give orders, or express strong emotions. The four possible sentence types are declarative, interrogative, imperative, and exclamatory.

Declarative: states an idea; ends with a period	Jacob sings in a choir.
Interrogative: asks a question; ends with a question mark	Where is the book?
Imperative: gives a command or makes a request; ends with a period or an exclamation point	Set the timer on the stove. Don't forget!
Exclamatory: conveys strong emotions; ends with an exclamation point	What a mystery that was!

PRACTICE A Punctuating the Four Types of Sentences

Read each sentence, and confirm that you understand its function (indicated in parentheses). Then, add the correct end mark.

Example: Why did the committee request a meeting (interrogative)
Answer: Why did the committee request a meeting?

1. What a wonderful story that was (exclamatory)
2. Please wash the vegetables (imperative)
3. Some mushrooms grow on stumps (declarative)
4. What are your expectations (interrogative)
5. The table is made of pine (declarative)
6. What an excellent idea she had (exclamatory)
7. Enter the information in your chart (imperative)
8. Dingoes are wild dogs (declarative)
9. Display parking permits on the windshield (imperative)
10. Can you name two aquatic insects (interrogative)

PRACTICE B Identifying the Four Types of Sentences

Read each sentence. Then, on the line provided, label the sentence declarative, interrogative, imperative, or exclamatory.

Example: Go to the top of the stairs and turn left.
Answer: imperative

1. The members of the committee all agreed.
_____

2. Turn down the volume, please. _____

3. How true that is! _____

4. Did you know that raccoons are nocturnal?
_____

5. What a funny story that was! _____

6. Wheat, rice, and corn are cereal grasses.

7. The northern lights are quite a sight.
_____

8. Which plants can live in arctic temperatures?
_____

9. Giraffes feed on acacia tree leaves.
_____

10. Notice the hooked bill on the flamingo.
_____

Writing and Speaking Application

Write a short description of an interesting event. Include declarative, interrogative, imperative, and exclamatory sentences. Read your description to a partner. Your partner should listen for and identify each type of sentence. Then, switch roles with your partner.

32 SENTENCE COMBINING

You can combine two short, choppy sentences by forming compound subjects, verbs, or objects or by forming compound or complex sentences.

This chart shows examples of ways in which two short, choppy sentences can be combined into one more-effective sentence.

Compound Subject	Alma plays video games. Marcos plays video games.	<u>Alma and Marcos</u> play video games.
Compound Verb	We mowed the lawn. We raked the leaves.	We <u>mowed the lawn and raked the leaves.</u>
Compound Object	Ling plays chess. Ling plays soccer.	Ling plays <u>chess and soccer.</u>
Compound Sentence	Most bears have varied diets. Pandas eat mainly bamboo.	Most bears have varied diets, <u>but pandas eat mainly bamboo.</u>
Complex Sentence	Angelo turned onto Main Street. Angelo parked the car.	<u>After Angelo turned onto Main Street,</u> he parked the car.

PRACTICE A Identifying Compound Subjects, Verbs, and Objects in Sentences

Read each sentence. Underline the compound subject, verb, or object.

Example: The committee proposed a new plan and discussed the details.

Answer: The committee <u>proposed a new plan and discussed the details</u>.

1. The hawksbill turtle lives in the sea and feeds on sponges.
2. Daffodils and crocuses are spring flowers.
3. Edgar Allan Poe wrote "The Black Cat" and "The Purloined Letter."
4. Langston Hughes and Sylvia Plath are famous poets.
5. Mars has a rocky core and a very thin atmosphere.
6. The waiter brought glasses of ice water and a basket of bread.
7. Angie appreciates literature and travel reviews.
8. Some authors write in metaphor and use symbolism.
9. Broccoli, cauliflower, and kale are part of the cabbage family.
10. After dinner, I explored my options and decided to attend a lecture.

PRACTICE B Distinguishing Compound Sentences and Complex Sentences

Read each sentence. On the line provided, write whether it is compound *or* complex.

Example: If you don't mind, I will schedule the meeting for tomorrow.

Answer: <u>complex</u>

1. Even though we were running late, we still made it to the bus stop on time. _____
2. Danny did not turn off the grill, so it ran out of propane gas. _____
3. Liselle ate the asparagus, but she considered it overcooked. _____
4. Hector has worn contacts since he was in eighth grade. _____
5. Although I have been there before, I don't remember how to get to the stadium. _____

Writing and Speaking Application

Write two sentences that relate to each other. Then, exchange papers with a partner. Your partner should combine these sentences and read the new sentence aloud. Then, switch roles with your partner.

33 VARYING SENTENCE LENGTH

Varying the lengths of your sentences can help you develop a rhythm, achieve an effect, or emphasize the connections between ideas.

Effective writers use a variety of sentence lengths. If your writing includes too many short, choppy sentences, consider combining two sentences by turning the ideas in one of the sentences into, for example, a prepositional phrase, a participial phrase, or a subordinate clause. If your writing includes too many long, complicated sentences, consider breaking up one of the sentences into two shorter sentences.

PRACTICE A Revising to Shorten Sentences

Read each sentence. Then, revise it by stating the ideas more directly.

Example: Our new television displays crisp images, and I appreciate those crisp images.
Answer: I appreciate the crisp images that our new television displays.

1. The oak has not lost its leaves yet, but all of the other trees have lost their leaves.

    _____

2. The peanut is not really a nut; botanically, it is in fact considered a legume like peas.

    _____

3. Many lives have been saved by seat belts because of mandatory seat-belt-use laws.

    _____

4. Most breeds of dogs shed a lot, but the standard poodle sheds very little.

    _____

5. Alan took his car through the carwash, but before he did that he filled it with gas.

    _____

PRACTICE B Revising to Vary Sentence Length

Read the following paragraph. Make these revisions to vary sentence length: Shorten sentence 1; combine sentences 2 and 3, and 4 and 5; break up sentence 7.

Example: Rio de Janeiro is the former capital of Brazil. It's also the second largest city.
Answer: Rio de Janeiro is the second largest city and the former capital of Brazil.

(1) The harbor of Rio de Janeiro is a natural wonder, one of the Seven Natural Wonders of the World. (2) It is located at Rio de Janeiro, Brazil. (3) The harbor was created by erosion from the ocean. (4) Its name came from the Portuguese navigators who found the harbor in January 1502 and believed it was the mouth of a river. (5) The name means "River of January." (6) There are many points from which to view the scenery that earned the harbor its status as a world wonder. (7) From the harbor, the panorama of surrounding mountains is amazing, and there are also views from the mountains, and they are equally stunning, with vistas of the harbor, the outlying islands, the city, and the tropical forests.

_____

_____

_____

Writing and Speaking Application

Write a paragraph about a current event. Make sure to vary the sentence length. Find a partner and take turns reading your paragraphs aloud.

Name _____ Date _____

34 VARYING SENTENCE BEGINNINGS

Varying the beginnings of your sentences can help you maintain your audience's interest.

Effective writers vary the ways in which they begin their sentences. When too many of your sentences begin with the subject of the sentence (a pronoun, a noun, or a noun phrase), your audience may lose interest. Consider beginning some of your sentences with elements such as adverbs, prepositional phrases, participial phrases, and infinitive phrases. This chart shows examples of various sentence beginnings:

Subject (Pronoun)	I went to soccer practice.
Adverb	Clearly, the problem is complex.
Prepositional Phrase	Before departure, I packed emergency supplies.
Participial Phrase	Concerned that I might be late, I left extra early.
Infinitive Phrase	To achieve my goals, I finally set a plan.

PRACTICE A Identifying Varied Sentence Beginnings

Each sentence below has an underlined sentence opening. Circle the answer in parentheses that accurately describes the underlined sentence opening.

Example: <u>Trying to remain calm</u>, Jan eased the car out of the ditch. (participial phrase / adverb)
Answer: (participial phrase / adverb)

1. <u>To get some answers</u>, I contacted consumer affairs. (infinitive phrase / participial phrase)

2. <u>Clearly</u>, Issa had prepared for the exam. (participial phrase / adverb)

3. <u>After the meeting</u>, we went to lunch. (prepositional phrase / participial phrase)

4. <u>Pleased with the results</u>, Laura displayed the painting. (participial phrase / prepositional phrase)

5. <u>Between the buildings</u>, the truck unloaded office supplies. (prepositional phrase / infinitive phrase)

6. <u>Paulo and Ada</u> lost track of time. (subject / participial phrase)

7. <u>Along the way</u>, we saw a woodpecker and two blue jays. (participial phrase / prepositional phrase)

8. <u>Gratefully</u>, Mr. Castillo accepted help with the bags of groceries. (participial phrase / adverb)

PRACTICE B Writing Varied Sentence Beginnings

On each line provided, complete the sentence by adding a word or phrase, using the part of speech or type of phrase indicated in parentheses.

Example: _____, Allen drew a sketch. (participial phrase)
Answer: <u>Doodling in his notebook</u>, Allen drew a sketch.

1. _____, Marco found the ingredients for the cake. (participial phrase)

2. _____, the carpenter shaped the wood to fit the frame. (adverb)

3. _____, something large was moving. (prepositional phrase)

4. _____, Camilla reviewed the data. (adverb)

5. _____ was his hope. (infinitive phrase)

Writing and Speaking Application

Write a sentence that begins with an adverb. Read your sentence to a partner. Your partner should restate your sentence, beginning with a different part of speech or with a phrase. Try to come up with several variations of your sentence. Then, switch roles with your partner.

Name _____ Date _____

35 USING INVERTED WORD ORDER

Word order in a sentence is *inverted* when the subject follows the verb.

Inverting word order is another way to make sentences more interesting. See the examples below.

Subject-Verb Order	A bunch of bananas sat in the bowl.
Verb-Subject Order	In the bowl sat a bunch of bananas.

PRACTICE A Identifying Subjects and Verbs in Sentences

Read each sentence. Underline the verb and circle the subject. (Not all the sentences have an inverted word order.)

Example: Extraordinary were the efforts of the rescue team.
Answer: Extraordinary <u>were</u> the (efforts) of the rescue team.

1. To the top of the tree flew the crow.

2. A pilot and several of the flight crew came down the ramp.

3. The parking attendant leaned out of the booth.

4. The news report about the UFO sighting appeared in all the headlines.

5. Located at the top of the screen is the Tools tab.

6. Down the slide went the laughing children.

7. Behind a stack of books was hidden the receipt that I needed.

8. Elegantly decorated cakes filled the bakery window.

9. Through the rain came the tow truck.

10. A committee of residents is organizing the Memorial Day parade.

PRACTICE B Identifying Inverted Word Order in Sentences

Read each sentence. If the sentence uses traditional, subject-verb word order, write S-V. If it uses inverted, verb-subject word order, write V-S.

Example: Strutting in the field is a turkey.
Answer: <u>V-S</u>

1. Wrestling over the football were some boys.

2. A pool of gravy covered the mashed potatoes.

3. Located in the park are two waterfalls.

4. The plates are above the dishwasher.

5. The early-morning swim was refreshing.

6. Around the hive flew a swarm of angry bees.

7. A magnolia tree blooms next to the pool.

8. Overtaking many lakes is the water hyacinth.

9. The Washington Monument is over there.

10. Entering the terminal are visitors from Iowa.

Writing and Speaking Application

Select four sentences from Practice A or Practice B that have traditional subject-verb word order. Rewrite the sentences, inverting the word order. Then, with a partner, take turns reading your sentences aloud.

36 RECOGNIZING FRAGMENTS

A sentence fragment is an incomplete sentence.

A fragment is a group of words that is missing a subject, a predicate, or both. One strategy for correcting a fragment is to connect it to words in a nearby sentence. Another strategy is to add any sentence parts that are needed to make the fragment a complete sentence.

This chart shows four examples of ways in which sentence fragments have been corrected:

Text That Includes a Fragment	Complete Sentence
Lindsay wants to buy a watch. Saw one in the window display.	Lindsay wants to buy the watch that she saw in the window display. (combined ideas using a relative clause)
Paolo had an interest in learning graphic design. Signed up for a class.	Interested in learning graphic design, Paolo signed up for a class. (combined ideas using a participial phrase)
The troupe of lively young dancers.	The troupe of lively young dancers moved gracefully across the stage. (added a predicate)
The troupe of lively young dancers.	The crowd applauded the troupe of lively young dancers. (added a subject; added a verb to create a predicate)

PRACTICE A Identifying Fragments

Read each item. If it is a fragment, *write* F *on the line provided. If it is a* complete sentence, *write* CS.

Example: Trays stacked neatly on the shelf.
Answer: F

1. Construction begins in May. _____
2. Lettie discovered a virus on her computer.
   _____
3. Pushing the wheelbarrow toward the house.
   _____
4. The art gallery in Soho's historic district.
   _____
5. After striking an agreement, we shook hands.
   _____

6. Before the orchestra started playing. _____
7. The chart listed animals native to the Amazon.
   _____
8. Store onions and potatoes in a cool place.
   _____
9. The dentist who extracted my tooth. _____
10. Enrollment was down for the pottery classes.
    _____

PRACTICE B Correcting Fragments

Read each fragment. Fill in the blank to form a complete sentence. Add punctuation as necessary.

Example: Because the poison ivy had spread _____.
Answer: Because the poison ivy had spread, <u>he called the doctor</u>.

1. The brown leather shoes _____ worn by Jared.

2. _____ proposed an alternate solution.

3. In the afternoon session about essay writing, _____.

4. _____ was discovered inside the storage closet.

5. Taking classes at the university _____.

Writing and Speaking Application

In a group, take turns reading your sentences from Practice B aloud. Then, work independently to rewrite four of the sentences.

37 AVOIDING RUN-ON SENTENCES

A run-on sentence is two or more sentences capitalized and punctuated as if they were a single sentence.

A **run-on** sentence occurs when two independent clauses are joined together in an improper way. Sometimes, there is no punctuation mark separating the clauses. Other times, there is only a comma separating the clauses. (This second type of run-on sentence is known as a **comma splice**.)
One way to correct a run-on sentence is to separate the independent clauses with a semicolon (and, when appropriate, a transitional word or phrase). Another way is to separate them with a comma and a coordinating conjunction. A third way is to turn one of the independent clauses into a subordinate clause by adding a subordinating conjunction or a relative pronoun. This chart shows examples of all three methods:

Run-On Sentence	Possible Corrections
The game went into overtime we couldn't stay to watch.	The game went into overtime; **unfortunately,** we couldn't stay to watch. The game went into overtime, **but** we couldn't stay to watch. **Although** the game went into overtime, we couldn't stay to watch.

PRACTICE A Revising to Eliminate Run-Ons

Read each item. Correct each run-on sentence by using one of the methods described above.

Example: I bought a new laptop it has much better resolution than my old one.
Answer: I bought a new laptop; it has much better resolution than my old one.

1. Mia suggested some fundraisers for example the art club might sell original artwork.
2. I read *Touching Spirit Bear* it is a book about a troubled teen who is reformed.
3. I usually eat a sizable dinner this week I haven't had much of an appetite.
4. Adriane writes for the school newspaper, she is always looking for a good story.
5. My dad is baking a pan of lasagna you are welcome to join us for dinner.
6. We wanted to go to the concert we could not get tickets.

PRACTICE B Rewriting to Eliminate Run-Ons

Read each item. Correct each run-on sentence by rewriting it.

Example: Karen purchased the microwave it was displayed on the bottom shelf.
Answer: Karen purchased the microwave that was displayed on the bottom shelf.

1. The ears on a Siamese cat look very large it has a triangular face.

   _____

2. I held my finger still, my mother removed the splinter of wood.

   _____

3. The roads were very icy, I drove slowly and with great caution.

   _____

4. George made all the arrangements, he wanted everything to be perfect.

   _____

5. Raj thought we had forgotten his birthday, we appeared with a cake and gifts.

   _____

Writing and Speaking Application

Take turns saying run-on sentences with a partner. Your partner should turn each run-on sentence into a single sentence and write it down. Then, switch roles with your partner. Trade papers and check that the sentences are correctly punctuated.

38 RECOGNIZING MISPLACED MODIFIERS

A misplaced modifier is placed too far from the word(s) it modifies, so it appears to modify the wrong word(s).

A misplaced modifier may be an individual word, such as an adjective or an adverb; a phrase, such as a prepositional phrase or a participial phrase; or an entire clause, such as a relative clause. When modifiers are misplaced, they can confuse your audience because they appear to modify the wrong words. To correct a misplaced modifier, move it closer to the word it modifies. See the example below, in which the modifier appears in boldface and the word it modifies is underlined.

Misplaced Modifier	Correction
A <u>man</u> walked by the store **talking loudly on a phone.**	A <u>man</u> **talking loudly on a phone** walked by the store.

PRACTICE A Identifying Misplaced Modifiers

Read each sentence. Underline the misplaced modifier, and circle the word(s) it is meant to modify.

Example: Cindy talked on the phone drinking tea.
Answer: (Cindy) talked on the phone <u>drinking tea</u>.

1. The man ran toward the bus holding a backpack.

2. Tina told me that it was too cold to go skiing during dinner.

3. Covered with mold, he threw the loaf of bread in the garbage.

4. Felix baked a cake in the oven flavored with nutmeg.

5. Hakim placed the essays in a manila folder that the class had written.

6. Javier posted the note on the refrigerator that his teacher had sent.

PRACTICE B Correcting Misplaced Modifiers

Read each sentence. Then, rewrite each sentence, putting the misplaced modifier closer to the word(s) it should modify.

Example: Aunt Shelly delivered a gift to my parents wrapped in silver paper.
Answer: <u>Aunt Shelly delivered a gift wrapped in silver paper to my parents.</u>

1. The midshipman boarded the aircraft carrier with short hair.

_____

2. Julio served fruit to his guests in cups.

_____

3. The kids walked to the parking lot after seeing a movie eating popcorn.

_____

4. Elias made several phone calls about his computer pacing across the room.

_____

5. Chopping carrots, the dog wagged its tail and barked at my mother.

_____

Writing and Speaking Application

Write four sentences describing a scene in a movie. Use modifiers in your sentences. Trade papers with a partner. Your partner should name the modifiers in your description and tell whether they are correctly placed. Then, switch roles with your partner.

39 RECOGNIZING DANGLING MODIFIERS

A dangling modifier seems to modify the wrong word or no word at all because an important word or words have been omitted from the sentence.

Correct a dangling modifier by adding missing words and making other needed changes. Look at the example below and ask, *Who is registering?* Is the word in the sentence on the left? Is it in the sentence on the right?

Dangling Modifier	Correction
Registering at the door, a higher price will be paid.	Registering at the door, **participants** will pay a higher price.

PRACTICE A Identifying Dangling Modifiers

*Read each pair of sentences. Put a check mark next to the sentence that does **not** have a dangling modifier.*

Example: a. While turning on the radio, the volume was too loud. _____
Answer: b. While turning on the radio, I made the volume too loud. _____✓_____

1. **a.** After running the bake sale, there was enough to buy a new computer. _____
   b. After running the bake sale, we made enough to buy a new computer. _____
2. **a.** To reserve a ticket, we had to wait in a long line, which was boring. _____
   b. To reserve a ticket, waiting in a long line was boring. _____
3. **a.** Born in Alaska, Georgia was too warm and humid. _____
   b. Born in Alaska, I found Georgia was too warm and humid. _____
4. **a.** After working in the hot sun, the lemonade tasted great. _____
   b. After I worked in the hot sun, the lemonade tasted great. _____

PRACTICE B Correcting Dangling Modifiers

Read each sentence. Then, rewrite each sentence, correcting any dangling modifiers by rearranging the words in the sentence and/or supplying missing words or ideas.

Example: Peeking around the corner, everyone is working on the assignment.
Answer: Peeking around the corner, I see everyone working on the assignment.

1. Sitting near the fireplace, the warmth was comforting.

_____

2. Clicking the red button, the file closed.

_____

3. After sitting down, the interview started.

_____

4. Cooking pasta, the water boiled over.

_____

Writing and Speaking Application

Write a sentence that contains a dangling modifier. Model your sentence on one of the incorrect sentences in Practice B. Rewrite the sentence to correct the dangling modifier, and read both sentences to a partner. Your partner should identify which sentence is incorrect. Then, switch roles with your partner.

40 RECOGNIZING THE CORRECT USE OF PARALLELISM

Parallelism involves presenting equal ideas in words, phrases, clauses, or sentences of similar types.

Parallel Words	The alleyway was **narrow, cluttered,** and **deserted.** (adjectives)
Parallel Phrases	It was **behind the diner** and **around the corner.** (prepositional phrases)
Parallel Clauses	That diner makes the famous sandwiches **that I constantly crave** and **that the hospital employees order often.** (relative clauses)
Parallel Sentences	**You can curse the darkness. You can light a candle instead.** (sentences with similar grammatical structures)

PRACTICE A Identifying Parallel Grammatical Structures

Read each sentence. Underline the parallel words, phrases, or clauses.

Example: The photograph of the waterfalls is blurry and dark.
Answer: The photograph of the waterfalls is <u>blurry</u> and <u>dark</u>.

1. Catawba, cantaloupe, and honeydew are all types of melons.

2. Some students attended both the science fair and the theater group performance.

3. After dinner I will write my essay and revise it.

4. My jacket has a hood, fleece lining, and black buttons.

5. Liam drove down the street where Jose lives and where Alena plays soccer.

6. Muhammad attends a local university; Emma goes to a college in Ohio.

7. Gary dropped off a bag of fresh tomatoes, and Dad used a couple in our salad.

8. To wash the car, I need the hose, a rag, and a bucket of soapy water.

9. Shana wants to learn how to write code and how to fix network systems.

10. Megan not only chopped the logs but also stacked them.

PRACTICE B Recognizing Parallel Grammatical Structures

To create a sentence with parallel structure, match each item on the left with the appropriate words on the right. The first sentence has been completed for you.

__E__ 1. After school, Edith attends play rehearsal	**A.** and to design highways.
_____ 2. John enjoys boating	**B.** but also the best pumpkin pie.
_____ 3. My dad makes not only the best bread	**C.** and I never will.
_____ 4. Enrique hopes to study engineering	**D.** and that everyone should own one.
_____ 5. Imani feels that cats are the best pets	**E.** and practices her flute.
_____ 6. I never thought it possible,	**F.** and water-skiing.

Writing and Speaking Application

Write four sentences with parallel ideas. Trade papers with a partner. Your partner should underline the parallel ideas. Take turns reading the sentences aloud.

41 CORRECTING FAULTY PARALLELISM

Faulty parallelism occurs when a writer uses unequal grammatical structures to express related ideas.

Nonparallel Words	Rhoda likes **hiking, running,** and **to ski.** (two gerunds vs. an infinitive; parallel = *skiing*)
Nonparallel Phrases	Harry is trying **to outrun Jim** and **kicking the ball into the net.** (infinitive phrase vs. gerund phrase; parallel = *to kick the ball into the net*)
Nonparallel Clauses	**I prefer memoirs and autobiographies,** whereas **fiction is preferred by my brother.** (active voice vs. passive voice; parallel = *my brother prefers fiction*)

PRACTICE A Identifying Faulty Parallelism

Read each sentence. Decide whether the underlined words are parallel. Write P *for parallel and* NP *for not parallel.*

Example: I have instructions <u>to store the tools in the shed</u> and <u>bringing out the mower.</u>
Answer: NP

1. The new shopping center has <u>two restaurants</u> and <u>there is a grocery store</u>. _____

2. <u>To buy some bait</u> and then <u>to bait a hook</u> is my plan. _____

3. Do you want <u>to take a train</u> or <u>driving</u> when we go on vacation? _____

4. Donna <u>likes to live in the city</u> but <u>doesn't like to take the subway</u>. _____

5. Let's go <u>to the store</u> and then <u>to the park</u>. _____

6. Edgardo plans <u>to ride the bus on Monday</u> and <u>walking the rest of the week</u>. _____

7. Ty picked pears from the tree that I <u>bought</u> and <u>planted</u> ten years ago. _____

8. The plan on the Fourth of July is <u>to eat barbecue</u> and <u>watching fireworks</u>. _____

9. The library has <u>ample lighting</u> and <u>comfortable chairs</u>. _____

10. First <u>waking up late</u> and then <u>to run out of hot water</u>—what a bad morning! _____

PRACTICE B Revising to Eliminate Faulty Parallelism

Read each sentence. Then, on the line provided, revise the underlined word or words to correct any faulty parallelism.

Example: The incident was reported by major newspapers and <u>newspapers that are small and local</u>.
Answer: small, local newspapers

1. I like biking and <u>to run</u>. _____

2. We need to stop for gas and <u>picking up</u> groceries on our way home. _____

3. This shirt is both warm and <u>it's stylish</u>. _____

4. My responsibilities include mowing the lawn and <u>to rake the leaves</u>. _____

5. The greatest achievement is to find happiness and then <u>keeping</u> it. _____

Writing and Speaking Application

Write four sentences with parallel ideas. Trade papers with a partner. You and your partner should check for correct use of parallelism. Take turns reading the sentences aloud.

42 CORRECTING FAULTY PARALLELISM IN A SERIES

Faulty parallelism in a series occurs when a writer lists items or ideas with unequal grammatical structures.

Nonparallel Structure	Correction
Amir likes to stir-fry, to grill, or **steaming** vegetables.	Amir likes to stir-fry, to grill, or **to steam** vegetables.
Kelly enjoys skateboarding, riding BMX, and **to read** novels.	Kelly enjoys skateboarding, riding BMX, and **reading** novels.

PRACTICE A Identifying Faulty Parallelism in a Series

Read each sentence. Underline the words in each series that are nonparallel.

Example: To add flair to a salad, toss in chopped nuts, diced fruit, or shred cheese.
Answer: To add flair to a salad, toss in chopped nuts, diced fruit, or <u>shredded cheese</u>.

1. Kirsten saves greeting cards, movie-ticket stubs, and she keeps hand-written letters.

2. Zayn expects that the musical will be lively, entertaining, and will have humor.

3. Some people think that the new theater is too big, too remote, and it won't get enough business.

4. Tyler's older brother is smart, funny, and has a quirky personality.

5. To shop wisely, you should make a list, stick to it, and sale products should be bought.

6. I have a cockatiel and an African gray parrot is also my pet.

7. Would you rather watch TV, take a walk in the park, or to play video games?

8. My responsibilities in the drama club include moving the set, getting props, and to help with costumes.

PRACTICE B Revising to Eliminate Faulty Parallelism in a Series

Read each sentence. Then, rewrite it to correct any nonparallel structures.

Example: Before you lock the doors, turn on the outside lights and the alarm must be set.
Answer: <u>Before you lock the doors, turn on the outside lights and set the alarm.</u>

1. At my part-time job, my duties include stocking the shelves, to sweep the floors, and taking out the trash.

_____

2. The toddler was crying, screaming, and kicked the floor.

_____

3. Ibrahim enjoys reading, hiking, and to bike.

_____

4. For this recipe, add milk, eggs, and flour should added.

_____

5. The fundraiser required organization, hard work, and being dedicated.

_____

Writing and Speaking Application

Write four sentences that have parallel series. Trade papers with a partner. Your partner should check for correct parallelism. Take turns reading the sentences aloud.

Name _____ Date _____

43 CORRECTING FAULTY PARALLELISM IN COMPARISONS

Faulty parallelism occurs when a writer uses nonparallel words, phrases, or clauses in comparisons.

In making comparisons, writers generally should compare a phrase with the same type of phrase and a clause with the same type of clause.

Nonparallel Structure	Correction
Many teens prefer texting to **a phone conversation.**	Many teens prefer texting to **talking on the phone.**

PRACTICE A Identifying Faulty Parallelism in a Comparison

Read each pair of sentences. Put a check mark next to the sentence with correct parallelism in a comparison.

Example: a. Shelby prefers music to taking drama. _____
Answer: b. Shelby prefers music to drama. ____✓____

1. **a.** I prefer salad to pasta. _____
    b. I prefer salad to eating pasta _____
2. **a.** My parents buy vegetables at the farmer's market rather than buying them at the grocery store. _____
    b. My parents buy vegetables at the farmer's market rather than at the grocery store. _____
3. **a.** I like watching movies more than seeing plays. _____
    b. I like watching movies more than going to see plays. _____
4. **a.** Amy did her research at the library instead of researching at home. _____
    b. Amy did her research at the library instead of at home. _____
5. **a.** Austin prefers reading a book to listening to an audiobook. _____
    b. Austin prefers reading a book to a book you listen to as an audiobook. _____

PRACTICE B Revising to Eliminate Faulty Parallelism in a Comparison

Read each sentence. Then, rewrite it to correct any faulty parallelism.

Example: Sophie swims the breaststroke just as well as she can do the butterfly.
Answer: Sophie swims the breaststroke just as well as she swims the butterfly.

1. Hyun prefers sparkling water to drinking lemonade.

    _____

2. Ashley chose a table instead of sitting in a booth.

    _____

3. We think shopping online is better than the mall.

    _____

4. He wrote more about being a fisherman than his time as a carpenter.

    _____

Writing and Speaking Application

Write several sentences in which you use parallel comparisons. Read your sentences to a partner. Your partner should note and correct any faulty parallelism. Then, switch roles with your partner.

Name _____ Date _____

44 RECOGNIZING FAULTY COORDINATION

When two or more independent clauses of unequal importance are joined by *and* or another coordinating conjunction, the result can be faulty coordination.

Faulty coordination occurs when two clauses are connected by a coordinating conjunction, but a subordinating conjunction, a relative pronoun, or a different coordinating conjunction would better express the relationship between the ideas in the two clauses. Consider the example in the chart:

| Faulty Coordination | Jessie didn't answer when I called, and she was talking to someone else. |
| Correct Coordination | Jessie didn't answer when I called because she was talking to someone else. |

PRACTICE A Recognizing Correct Coordination and Subordination
Read each item. Match each item on the left with the words on the right that best complete the sentence, using correct coordination or subordination. The first item has been completed for you.

___B___ 1. Even though Jude was busy,

_____ 2. After he caught the pass,

_____ 3. As she smiled broadly,

_____ 4. Heidi offered to give us a ride,

_____ 5. Nathan pushed the car

_____ 6. I wanted to wear my purple shirt,

A. Khalil scored a touchdown.

B. she took time to talk to me.

C. Mrs. Lee greeted her friends at the door.

D. but it's in the laundry.

E. while Timo steered it off the road.

F. and we accepted her offer.

PRACTICE B Recognizing Faulty Coordination
Read each sentence. If it has faulty coordination, write FC. If it does not have faulty coordination, write correct.

Example: Frank is leaving now, and he has several other obligations this evening.
Answer: FC

1. My uncle teaches at the high school, and it is down the road. _____

2. A storm had come through earlier, so branches were scattered all over the yard. _____

3. We try not to disturb the robins, and they are nesting on our patio. _____

4. Abeni enjoyed the dinosaur exhibit even though she didn't get to see everything. _____

5. My cousins and I don't see each other often, and they live in another state. _____

6. Yusef was accepted to college and received a full scholarship. _____

7. Ross pulled up the blinds, and he wanted to see what was clanging outside. _____

8. We saw Bridal Veil Falls, which are on the American side of Niagara Falls. _____

9. Ms. Nidel loves gardening, and she lives two houses up the street from us. _____

10. I have always loved cats and dogs, and I am highly allergic to them. _____

Writing and Speaking Application
Write two sentences that contain faulty coordination. Have a partner read your sentences and correct the faulty coordination. Read the original sentences and revised sentences aloud and note the differences.

45 CORRECTING FAULTY COORDINATION

Faulty coordination is caused by an unclear relationship between clauses and can be corrected by making the relationship between those clauses clear.

Faulty Coordination	The tundra is a unique habitat, and it has many interesting plants.
Divided Into Two Sentences	The tundra is a unique habitat. Many interesting plants grow there.
One Clause Subordinated	The tundra is a unique habitat where many interesting plants grow.
One Clause Changed to a Phrase	The tundra, a unique habitat, has many interesting plants.

PRACTICE A Revising to Eliminate Faulty Coordination

Read each sentence. Then, show how you would begin to create two sentences to correct the faulty coordination: Draw a vertical line where the first sentence would end.

Example: Eric wrote an article about holidays, and I like Arbor Day.
Answer: Eric wrote an article about holidays, | and I like Arbor Day.

1. Felix carefully prepared the meal, and there are guests coming to dinner.

2. Juliana's stories are always funny, and she has a good sense of humor.

3. I spend hours doing my homework, and I left it on the table.

4. Students may choose the session that they want to attend, and the first one is today.

5. Mr. Patel is at the front door, and the back door has no doorbell.

PRACTICE B Using Subordination to Eliminate Faulty Coordination

Read each sentence. Then, rewrite it, changing the less important idea into a phrase or a subordinate clause.

Example: Tessa does an Italian dance, and the dance is called the *tarantella*.
Answer: Tessa does an Italian dance called the *tarantella*.

1. Isabella announced her engagement, and it was during a family gathering.

   _____

2. Snow fell onto the branches of the hemlock, and it snowed big, fluffy clumps.

   _____

3. Uncle Cliff will take a taxi to our house, and he just arrived at the airport.

   _____

4. The reporter interviewed the shop owners, and they were affected by the construction.

   _____

5. Lucille Clifton wrote "Fury," and she is the poet whom we read about last week.

   _____

Writing and Speaking Application

Choose two sentences from Practice B. Correct the faulty coordination by rewriting each sentence as two separate sentences. Trade papers with a partner and check each other's work. Then, take turns reading the revised sentences aloud.

Name _____ Date _____

46 THE SIMPLE AND PERFECT FORMS OF VERBS

In the present, past, and future tenses, verbs have both simple forms and perfect forms.

This chart shows the simple and perfect forms of the irregular verb *know*. Notice that the perfect forms of the verb all include a form of the helping verb *have*.

(Simple) Present	I know	Present Perfect	I have known
(Simple) Past	I knew	Past Perfect	I had known
(Simple) Future	I will know	Future Perfect	I will have known

PRACTICE A Identifying Verb Forms

Read each sentence. Write the form (present, past, future, present perfect, past perfect, or future perfect) of each underlined verb or verb phrase. Note that different verb forms may be used within a single sentence.

Example: Joy had completed all of her math requirements by the time she was a senior.
Answer: past perfect; past

1. Cruz checked off each item on the list as he threw it into the shopping cart. _____

2. Tanya will compare the results after she enters the rest of the data. _____

3. Once Anita had sliced the onions, she arranged them on a plate. _____

4. Jake will have tried every entree on the menu if he orders the shrimp. _____

5. I will see Seneca when she comes home at five. _____

6. My mother has competed in a local marathon every year in the last decade. _____

7. Rita had written down the wrong time, so she missed the meeting. _____

8. So far, I have found only two words in your essay that are misspelled. _____

9. Kelly drives an old car that her uncle gave her. _____

10. Mary Lou is home sick, so I will give our presentation without her. _____

PRACTICE B Revising Verb Forms

Read each sentence. Then, on the line provided, rewrite the underlined verb or verb phrase, using the verb form indicated in parentheses.

Example: Lizzy practiced taking foul shots to improve her skill. (present perfect)
Answer: has practiced

1. Aran turned in his homework assignment a day before it was due. (past perfect) _____

2. My brother traveled home from college by bus for semester breaks. (present) _____

3. Brooke completed the graph before the beginning of class. (future perfect) _____

4. Your determination to achieve your goals impresses me. (past) _____

5. This grading period ends at the end of next week. (future) _____

Writing and Speaking Application

Write a paragraph about a recent holiday. Use all six verb forms in your paragraph. Then, find a partner and take turns reading your paragraphs aloud.

Name _____ Date _____

47 THE FOUR PRINCIPAL PARTS OF VERBS

A verb has four principal parts: the present, the present participle, the past, and the past participle.

The chart below shows the principal parts of the regular verb *work* and the irregular verb *drive*.

Present	Present Participle	Past	Past Participle
work	working	worked	[have] worked
drive	driving	drove	[have] driven

PRACTICE A Recognizing the Four Principal Parts of Verbs

Read each set of words. Find the verb that is in the form indicated in parentheses. Write the verb and its present tense form.

Example: inspire, illustrated, catching (present participle)
Answer: <u>catching; catch</u>

1. scoop, swimming, judged (past)
   _____

2. crumbling, [have] suggested, commute (present participle) _____

3. understanding, contrast, baked (past)
   _____

4. allow, gathering, questioned (past)
   _____

5. attempting, [have] supported, waste (past participle) _____

6. produce, emerging, [have] welcomed (past participle) _____

7. prowl, absorbing, occurred (present participle)
   _____

8. screech, wrapping, [have] identified (past participle) _____

9. receiving, [have] advised, accept (present participle) _____

10. fluttered, improving, predict (present participle) _____

PRACTICE B Using the Four Principal Parts of Verbs

Read each sentence. Then, on the line provided, rewrite the underlined verb, using the principal part indicated in parentheses. You will need to add a form of the helping verb be *to use the present participles, and a form of the helping verb* have *to use the past participles.*

Example: Mr. Crane <u>is recording</u> the student presentations. (past)
Answer: <u>recorded</u>

1. The copperhead snake <u>slithered</u> toward the rock ledge. (present) _____

2. The cement truck <u>is pouring</u> concrete into wooden frames. (past) _____

3. Concerned, the doctor <u>ordered</u> an X-ray of my sister's knee. (past participle) _____

4. The lifeguards <u>have closed</u> the beach because of an incoming storm. (past) _____

5. The chipmunks <u>are chasing</u> each other along the split-rail fence. (present) _____

6. The students <u>debated</u> about the changes in the school dress code. (past participle) _____

7. My grandparents <u>have driven</u> through every state in the country. (present participle) _____

8. Billy <u>is helping</u> Mom take groceries into the house before dinner. (past) _____

Writing and Speaking Application

Write a paragraph describing an activity. Then, trade papers with a partner. Your partner should replace the principal parts of five verbs. Take turns reading the paragraphs aloud.

Name _____ Date _____

48 REGULAR AND IRREGULAR VERBS

Regular verbs form the past and past participle by adding *-ed* or *-d* to the present form (and sometimes doubling the final consonant). Irregular verbs do not use a predictable pattern to form their past and past participles.

This chart shows the principal parts of three regular verbs and three irregular verbs:

	Regular Verb	Regular Verb	Regular Verb	Irregular Verb	Irregular Verb	Irregular Verb
Present	feature	signal	wrap	run	choose	see
Present Participle	featuring	signaling	wrapping	running	choosing	seeing
Past	featured	signaled	wrapped	ran	chose	saw
Past Participle	(have) featured	(have) signaled	(have) wrapped	(have) run	(have) chosen	(have) seen

PRACTICE A Matching Present and Past Forms of Irregular Verbs

Match the present form of each verb on the left with the past form of the verb on the right. The first item has been completed for you.

F	1. sleep		**A.** wrote
_____	2. forgive		**B.** caught
_____	3. write		**C.** forgave
_____	4. hide		**D.** rode
_____	5. make		**E.** hid
_____	6. pay		**F.** slept
_____	7. ride		**G.** made
_____	8. bite		**H.** bit
_____	9. buy		**I.** bought
_____	10. catch		**J.** paid

PRACTICE B Using Principal Parts of Verbs in Sentences

Read each sentence. Then, write the principal part of a verb that makes sense in the sentence.

Example: Angelo _____ his collection of baseball cards online.
Answer: sold

1. Maya _____ the car's trunk to load the groceries.

2. I am _____ a book about whale migration.

3. Mrs. Khan _____ Adele that her paper is missing a title page.

4. That helicopter _____ over the house several times in the last hour.

5. Denise and I have _____ each other since we were toddlers.

Writing and Speaking Application

With a partner, take turns saying sentences with irregular verbs. Your partner should listen for and identify the forms of the verbs that you use and then write four sentences using those verbs. Then, switch roles.

Name _____ Date _____

49 THE PROGRESSIVE FORMS OF VERBS

The progressive forms of verbs are used to show ongoing actions or conditions.

To create a progressive form of a verb, use a form of the helping verb *be* plus the present participle of the main verb. This chart shows the progressive forms of the verb *walk*—both the simple and perfect forms of the present, past, and future tenses.

Present Progressive	I am walking	Present Perfect Progressive	I have been walking
Past Progressive	I was walking	Past Perfect Progressive	I had been walking
Future Progressive	I will be walking	Future Perfect Progressive	I will have been walking

PRACTICE A Recognizing Progressive Forms of Verbs

Read each sentence. Then, underline the progressive verb form in the sentence. Make sure you include any helping verbs that help create the progressive verb form.

Example: Rain has been falling for about two hours.
Answer: Rain <u>has been falling</u> for about two hours.

1. The defendant felt optimistic because talented attorneys were working on her case.

2. The performance will be starting in twenty minutes.

3. Experts have been testifying before the Senate all week.

4. A celebrated chef is preparing a three-course meal for the lucky diners.

5. Until moments before the guests arrived, we had been cleaning the entranceway.

6. Tomorrow, students will have been studying this topic for two full weeks.

PRACTICE B Writing Progressive Forms of Verbs

Read each sentence. Then, rewrite the sentence, using the progressive verb form indicated in parentheses.

Example: We walk. (future perfect progressive)
Answer: <u>We will have been walking.</u>

1. We listen. (present perfect progressive) _____

2. I dream. (past progressive) _____

3. They prepare. (future progressive) _____

4. She enjoys lunch. (present progressive) _____

5. You leap. (past progressive) _____

6. We travel. (future perfect progressive) _____

7. You skate. (past perfect progressive) _____

8. He buys. (past progressive) _____

Writing and Speaking Application

Write five sentences in which you use a progressive form of a verb. Read your sentences aloud to a partner. Your partner should identify the progressive verb form in each sentence. Then, switch roles with your partner.

Name _____ Date _____

50 USING VARIOUS VERB FORMS

Both action verbs and linking verbs have many forms. Learning to recognize and create the various forms of verbs will help you express your ideas clearly.

This chart shows the simple, progressive, perfect, and perfect progressive forms of the irregular action verb *see*—in the present, past, and future tenses.

Present	I see (simple), I am seeing (progressive), I have seen (perfect), I have been seeing (perfect progressive)
Past	I saw (simple), I was seeing (progressive), I had seen (perfect), I had been seeing (perfect progressive)
Future	I will see (simple), I will be seeing (progressive), I will have seen (perfect), I will have been seeing (perfect progressive)

PRACTICE A Identifying Verb Forms

Read each sentence. Then, on the line provided, identify the form of the verb underlined in the sentence.

Example: Miriam <u>will have forgotten</u> by the time she gets home.
Answer: future perfect

1. The boss <u>was training</u> Kyle to use the forklift.
_____

2. Harriet <u>has been driving</u> all morning.
_____

3. Dimitri <u>has been studying</u> since breakfast.
_____

4. Elise <u>is attempting</u> to figure out the problem.
_____

5. The students <u>applauded</u> their efforts.
_____

6. Jacob <u>will be arriving</u> by train in two hours.
_____

7. The president <u>will introduce</u> the speaker soon.
_____

8. Kimberly <u>solved</u> the math problem.
_____

9. The owner <u>had permitted</u> us to pick berries.
_____

10. The house <u>appears</u> to have been abandoned.
_____

PRACTICE B Supplying Verb Forms

Read each sentence. Then, complete the sentence by filling in the blank with the verb and form indicated in parentheses.

Example: I _____ mounting strips for the posters next week. (*buy*, future progressive)
Answer: I <u>will be buying</u> mounting strips for the posters next week.

1. Craig _____ at the gas station on the way over. (*stop*, past)

2. Nadine _____ dinner by now. (*finish*, future perfect)

3. The tire _____ flat by the time I noticed it. (*go*, past perfect)

4. Marco _____ to the store. (*walk*, present progressive)

5. I _____ you to Carmen's house. (*follow*, future progressive)

6. The wind _____ all night long. (*howl*, past perfect progressive)

Writing and Speaking Application

Write a short paragraph in which you use a variety of verb forms. Read your paragraph aloud to a partner. Your partner should listen for and identify the form of each verb you used. Then, switch roles with your partner.

51 SEQUENCE OF TENSES

When a sentence has more than one verb, the sequence of tenses of those verbs must be consistent with the time order in which events happen in the sentence.

Verb tenses help show *when* events happen, as well as *the order in which* they happen. When you encounter a sentence with multiple verbs, think about the time order in which the events must logically occur. Sometimes, the different tenses of the verbs will be a clue to the order of events. Other times, the verbs may have the same tense, yet there is still a logical order in which the events must happen.

In each of the examples in the chart, the verb expressing the event that occurs earlier in time is underlined:

I **went** to the market today, and I **purchased** a basil plant. (same tense; first verb describes earlier event)
Before I **made** lunch today, I **listened** to a new album. (same tense; second verb describes earlier event)
I **will watch** the movie with you after I **prepare** dinner. (different tenses; second verb describes earlier event)

PRACTICE A Identifying Time Sequence in Sentences With More Than One Verb

Read each sentence. Write the verb or the verb phrase of the event that happens <u>second</u> in time order.

Example: Lou will help you with your assignment if you meet him in the library.
Answer: will help

1. I looked up and saw my brother near the doorway. _____

2. Sal told me that Mr. Bosco will be arriving soon. _____

3. Dana added the vegetable oil after she measured it. _____

4. I wanted to attend the concert until I noticed the ticket price. _____

5. I have missed my best friend since she moved away. _____

6. Carol realized that she had forgotten her book in her locker. _____

7. Lisa called and asked for a ride home from work. _____

8. Please call the doctor's office and schedule an appointment. _____

9. We ran out of time, so we postponed our trip to the park. _____

10. Hank was upset that he had missed a call from his grandparents. _____

PRACTICE B Correcting Errors in Tense Sequence

Read each sentence. Then, rewrite the underlined verb to correct the error in tense sequence.

Example: Mira walks into the classroom and <u>set</u> down her backpack.
Answer: sets

1. The rosebush <u>blooms</u>, and the flowers gave off a delicate, spicy scent. _____

2. The glass <u>slips</u> out of Janice's hand and hit the floor with a crash. _____

3. Amara looked out the door and <u>sees</u> a squirrel sitting on the steps. _____

4. After we <u>arrived</u> at the campground, we will check in at the office. _____

5. Min-joon <u>puts</u> a stamp on the envelope and placed it in the mailbox. _____

Writing and Speaking Application

Write four sentences with correct tense sequence about a recent news story. Then, read the sentences to a partner. Your partner should listen for and identify the sequence of events in your sentences, correcting your verbs if necessary. Then, switch roles.

Name _____ Date _____

52 SIMULTANEOUS EVENTS

Simultaneous events are events that happen at the same time.

Some sentences with two or more verbs express events that happen simultaneously, or at the same time. Sometimes, a subordinating conjunction, such as *as*, *when*, or *while*, will signal that the events are simultaneous. Other times, the context of the sentence will reveal that the events must logically occur at the same time.

This chart shows examples of simultaneous events occurring in the present, in the past, and in the future:

In Present Time	Ava **hums** along as she **listens** to the song.
In Past Time	Ava **hummed** along as she **listened** to the song.
In Future Time	Ava **will hum** along as she **listens** to the song. (Notice that the *present tense* is often used to show *future time*, particularly in subordinate clauses.)

PRACTICE A Identifying Simultaneous Events in Sentences

Read each sentence. Underline the two verbs or verb phrases that indicate simultaenous events.

Example: As Julio was waiting in line patiently, he heard a subway train in the distance.
Answer: As Julio <u>was waiting</u> in line patiently, he <u>heard</u> a subway train in the distance.

1. When Joanne exercises, she listens to the news.

2. The calender indicates that Troy is visiting his cousins.

3. While Angie gathered her hair into a ponytail, she looked for a hair tie.

4. They paid attention as the instructor explained the lesson.

5. The end of summer vacation is approaching, and I feel a bit sad.

6. When my favorite song plays on the radio, I always sing along.

7. Christopher was carrying a bag of gifts as he strolled down the hallway to the celebration.

8. As the announcements came over the loudspeaker, Danny hurried to his locker.

PRACTICE B Completing Sentences About Simultaneous Events

Read each sentence. Then, using the line provided, complete the sentence by adding a verb or a verb phrase to indicate a simultaneous event.

Example: Brianna _____ at the library and saves money for her car insurance.
Answer: <u>works</u>

1. When I _____ a final goodbye to a friend who is moving, I cry.

2. While Devon talked on the phone, he _____ fetch with his dog.

3. Mr. Ortiz plays with his keys or jingles coins when he _____ impatient.

4. As the sun slowly _____ on the horizon, the lights of the city came on one by one.

5. I watched Shreya as she _____ up the path to the picnic table.

Writing and Speaking Application

Write four sentences to read to a partner about a recent experience. Each sentence should mention two simultaneous events. Your partner should listen for and identify the verbs and correct any errors in tense. Then, switch roles with your partner.

53 SEQUENTIAL EVENTS

Sequential events are chronological—an initial event is followed by one or more events.

In Present Time	She **listens** to the song and then **buys** the album.
In Past Time	She **listened** to the song and then **bought** the album.
Spanning Past and Future Time	She **listened** to the song and soon **will buy** the album.

PRACTICE A Identifying Sequential Events in Sentences

Read each sentence. Then, write the verb or verb phrase of the event that happens <u>first</u> in time order.

Example: If you see Sharon, will you ask her to stop by my house on her way home?
Answer: <u>see</u>

1. Terrance felt energized after he ran this morning. _____

2. Henry noticed that a tree had fallen during last night's storm. _____

3. Rhoda bought a book about birds so that she could identify the birds at her feeder. _____

4. Athena's parents saw her expression and realized that she had liked their gift. _____

5. You can find the most gas-efficient route if you get directions online. _____

6. Ruth was wondering why John had been frowning, so she asked him if he wanted to talk. _____

7. Donna opened the pantry and saw that something had spilled on the shelf. _____

8. I will call the number on the bottom of the ad and will make an appointment. _____

9. After you eat lunch, put your dishes in the dishwasher and wipe the table. _____

10. As soon as I have fixed this flat tire, I can eat dinner. _____

PRACTICE B Revising Sentences to Indicate Sequential Events

Complete each sentence so that a logical sequence of events is shown.

Example: Aya filled a bucket with soapy water _____
Answer: <u>and then washed the car.</u>

1. Mr. Goldmann opened the fridge _____

2. Once the rain had stopped, _____

3. My dog Lucky jumped onto my lap _____

4. After mixing all of the ingredients together, Mr. Li _____

5. As soon as Felicia had saved up enough money, _____

Writing and Speaking Application

Write three sentences that do not follow a logical sequence of events. Have your partner listen as your read your sentences aloud. Then, have your partner identify changes to verb tense that would create a logical sequence of events. Finally, switch roles with your partner.

54 MODIFIERS THAT HELP CLARIFY TIME

Adverbs and adverbial phrases can clarify the time expressed by a verb.

Modifiers can help clarify whether events occur in the past, in the present, or in the future. They also can help clarify whether events happen regularly, continuously, or at one particular time. Compare the sentences in the examples below.

Adverbs	Ralph washes his car **weekly**. Nate washed his car **yesterday**.
Adverbial Phrases	Al walks to school **every day**. Al jogged to the park **last week**.

PRACTICE A Identifying Modifiers That Help Clarify Time

Read each sentence. Then, underline the modifier that helps clarify the time expressed by the verb.

Example: Judith's cat had kittens this morning.
Answer: Judith's cat had kittens <u>this morning</u>.

1. This evening, we will be going to a fireworks display.

2. Suddenly, the lights flickered and then went out.

3. We eat dinner together as a family daily.

4. Once in a while, I make a bowl of hot cereal.

5. Never do I miss an opportunity to go to the skatepark.

6. I always drink water with my meals.

7. By next week, I will have saved enough money to buy a new pair of boots.

8. My brother texts me often with updates about what he's doing at college.

9. Tosha and I occasionally meet to study.

10. Every evening, I help cook dinner.

PRACTICE B Recognizing Modifiers That Help Clarify Time

Read each sentence. Then, fill in the modifier that best clarifies the time expressed by the verb. The first item has been completed for you.

often   recently   rarely   every morning   within a month   after dark

1. Josie <u>rarely</u> forgets anyone's name.

2. The deer come out to feed _____.

3. I take a long, hot shower _____.

4. I _____ misplace my keys.

5. She expects to have a new job _____.

6. Sophia _____ read that book.

Writing and Speaking Application

Write four sentences about events that took place in the past. Use modifiers to clarify tense. Then, change the modifiers and tell a partner about the events as if they will take place in the future. Your partner should listen for and identify the modifiers in your sentences. Then, switch roles.

55 USING THE SUBJUNCTIVE MOOD

The *subjunctive* mood can be used to express a request, a demand, or a proposal. It can also be used to express an idea that is contrary to fact.

There are three **moods**, or ways in which a verb can express an action or a condition: *indicative, imperative,* and *subjunctive.* The **indicative mood**, which is the most common, is used to make factual statements (*She is helpful.*) and to ask questions (*Is she helpful?*). The **imperative mood** is used to give orders or directions (*Be helpful.*).

The third mood, the **subjunctive mood**, can be used in two ways: (1) Use the subjunctive mood in a clause beginning with *that* to express a request, a demand, or a proposal. (2) Use the subjunctive mood in a clause beginning with *if* or *that* to express an idea that is contrary to fact.

To form the subjunctive, follow these rules: First, in a clause expressing a request, a demand, or a proposal, use the base form of the verb, even if the subject is third-person singular. Second, in a clause expressing an idea contrary to fact, the subjunctive mood of the verb *be* is were, regardless of the subject.

This chart shows two examples of verbs in the subjunctive mood:

To Express a Proposal	I suggest that he **attend** the lecture. (not *attends*)
To Express an Idea Contrary to Fact	If Mia **were** here, we could finish the project. (not *was*)

PRACTICE A Identifying Verb Mood

Read each sentence. Identify the mood of the underlined verb as indicative, imperative, *or* subjunctive.

Example: The administrator prefers that no one <u>skip</u> this meeting.
Answer: <u>subjunctive</u>

1. <u>Walk</u> faster!

   _____

2. The gray whale <u>is</u> a mammal.

   _____

3. If the store <u>were</u> open, I'd buy shoes.

   _____

4. Greg suggests that she <u>drive</u> separately.

   _____

5. <u>Do</u> you <u>recognize</u> the girl in the corner?

   _____

6. If Dakota <u>were</u> here, he would know!

   _____

7. <u>Be</u> prepared for the upcoming storm.

   _____

8. I wish that I <u>were</u> able to attend the concert.

   _____

PRACTICE B Recognizing the Subjunctive Mood

Read each sentence. Then, on the line provided, write the verb that is in the subjunctive mood.

Example: If I were less annoyed, I might be more patient.
Answer: <u>were</u>

1. If Katina were class president, things would improve quickly. _____
2. If he isn't feeling better, Ronnie may suggest that Lee take his place. _____
3. The director requested that the cast assemble for a meeting in an hour. _____
4. I wish that the weather were better for today's picnic. _____
5. The local paper requires that letters to the editor be short and to the point. _____

Writing and Speaking Application

Write several sentences similar to those in Practice B. Trade papers with a partner. Your partner should point out each subjunctive verb and tell what the verb is used to express.

56 AUXILIARY VERBS THAT EXPRESS THE SUBJUNCTIVE MOOD

Because certain auxiliary verbs (*could, would, should*) suggest conditions contrary to fact, they can often be used with a main verb to express the subjunctive mood in a clause beginning with *if*.

This chart shows an example of how, when a clause begins with *if*, the subjunctive mood can be expressed either by a form of the verb *to be* or by an auxiliary verb plus a main verb.

Expressed by a Form of *to be*	If Jared **were** here, he'd help me.
Expressed by an Auxiliary Verb	If Jared **could be** here, he'd help me.

PRACTICE A Identifying Auxiliary Verbs That Express the Subjunctive Mood

Read each sentence. Then, on the line provided, write the auxiliary verb that is used with a main verb to express the subjunctive mood in a clause beginning with if.

Example: If you would lend me your book, I'd return it quickly.
Answer: would

1. If I could move the large rocks, I'd plant a garden. _____

2. We'd study if Tamara would turn down the music. _____

3. If we should need help piling the lumber, would you give us a hand? _____

4. If the cabin could be made larger, we'd live there. _____

5. If Jose could be here, they'd ask for his help. _____

PRACTICE B Supplying Auxiliary Verbs to Express the Subjunctive Mood

Read each sentence. Then, rewrite the sentence, using an auxiliary verb plus a main verb to express the subjunctive mood in the clause beginning with if.

Example: The bikes could be stored in the garage if there were room.
Answer: The bikes could be stored in the garage if there should be room.

1. If I were to buy a new car, I'd buy a red sports car.

_____

2. Mark would copy his notes for me if I were absent.

_____

3. If I were to learn to golf, I'd be good at it. _____

4. If he were to arrive on time, I'd be shocked. _____

5. I'd see you if you were to stop by before I go to work.

_____

6. We'd be hungry before dinner if we were to eat now.

Writing and Speaking Application

Write a paragraph describing something that you wish would happen. Use auxiliary verbs along with main verbs to express the subjunctive mood. With a partner, take turns reading your paragraphs aloud. Your partner should identify your uses of the subjunctive mood.

Name _____ Date _____

57 ACTIVE AND PASSIVE VOICE

The *voice* of a verb shows whether the subject is performing the action of the verb or is receiving the action of the verb.

Active voice shows that the subject is performing an action. **Passive voice** shows that the subject is having an action performed on it. To create the passive voice, use a form of the helping verb *be* plus the past participle of the main verb. If you wish to indicate the performer of the action, introduce the performer with the preposition *by*, as in the example below.

Active Voice	Jamal **attended** the surprise party.
Passive Voice	The surprise party **was attended** by Jamal.

PRACTICE A Identifying Active and Passive Voice

Read each sentence. Decide whether the underlined verb is written in active or passive voice. Write AV *for active voice or* PV *for passive voice.*

Example: Lindsay <u>worked</u> an eight-hour shift.
Answer: <u>AV</u>

1. The raccoon <u>scampered</u> into the woods. _____
2. The song <u>was sung</u> by Alicia. _____
3. The house <u>was built</u> by James. _____
4. Mrs. Steiner <u>visited</u> Spain. _____
5. Dante <u>scrubbed</u> the floor. _____

6. The artwork <u>is being exhibited</u> by Ty. _____
7. Penguins <u>inhabit</u> polar climates. _____
8. Clouds <u>floated</u> across the blue sky. _____
9. The windows <u>were washed</u> by Jake. _____
10. The violin <u>is being played</u> by Carlos. _____

PRACTICE B Rewriting in Active Voice

Reach each sentence. Then, rewrite each sentence in active voice.

Example: Tomatoes were picked by Phoebe.
Answer: <u>Phoebe picked tomatoes.</u>

1. The shrubs were planted by George. _____
2. It was bought by my aunt Clarissa. _____
3. A big sign was installed by the township. _____
4. Carrots for the soup were chopped by the cook. _____
5. The meeting was arranged by the manager. _____
6. A shopping list was written by my dad. _____
7. Their singing was applauded by the audience. _____
8. The brochure was illustrated by an artist. _____
9. The mail was set on the counter by Theresa. _____
10. Work boots were arranged in a display by Mr. Zhang. _____

Writing and Speaking Application

Write four sentences about what you did last weekend. Use both active voice and passive voice. Next, read the sentences to a partner. Have your partner identify the voice of each sentence. Finally, switch roles with your partner.

58 USING ACTIVE AND PASSIVE VOICE

In general, use of active voice makes for stronger writing. However, writers may use passive voice when they want to emphasize the receiver of an action, or when the performer of an action is unimportant or is not easily identified.

This chart shows two examples of appropriate uses of passive voice:

Angela **was escorted** to her seat. (emphasizes the receiver of the action, *Angela*)
The performance's sponsors **were listed** in the program. (the performer of the action is not easily identified)

PRACTICE A Recognizing the Performer of an Action

Read each sentence. Then, on the line provided, write the performer of the action.

Example: The horse drank water from the trough.
Answer: <u>horse</u>

1. Harry was introduced to the family by my grandmother. _____

2. Kay was spoken to by the bank teller. _____

3. An alligator swam across the brackish swamp. _____

4. DeShawn ordered a grilled cheese sandwich. _____

5. The baseball was hit out of the stadium by Frank. _____

6. The walls were being painted by a contractor. _____

7. Marissa measured the board and used a saw to cut it. _____

8. Waves crashed against the rickety dock. _____

PRACTICE B Using Active Voice

Read each item, then use the subject and the verb to write a sentence in active voice.

Example: Jude and Keisha—planned
Answer: <u>Jude and Keisha planned to attend the same college.</u>

1. two mallard ducks—swam _____

2. clusters of tomatoes—ripened _____

3. cars—filled _____

4. Vic—parked _____

5. the eagle—swooped _____

6. Maria—studied _____

7. The dog—ran _____

8. Mr. Ableman—listened _____

9. Taylor—bought _____

10. Mrs. Hussain—walked _____

Writing and Speaking Application

Write a paragraph about activities members of your family did this past week. Trade papers with a partner. Your partner should underline the performer of the action in each sentence. Then, take turns saying sentences about activities you enjoy, using active voice.

59 PRONOUN CASE

Case is the form of a pronoun that shows how it is used in a sentence. The three cases of pronouns are the nominative, the objective, and the possessive.

This chart shows the nominative, objective, and possessive forms of personal and possessive pronouns:

Case	Example Sentence
Nominative: I, we, you, it, he, she, they	<u>He</u> went to the park.
Objective: me, us, you, it, him, her, them	The teacher gave <u>her</u> the book.
Possessive: my, mine, our, ours, your, yours, its, his, her, hers, their, theirs	The bike is <u>mine</u>.

PRACTICE A Identifying Pronouns

Read each sentence. Then, underline each pronoun.

Example: They went on a picnic.
Answer: <u>They</u> went on a picnic.

1. Give them the answer.
2. Our younger sister surprised us.
3. Your short story is more interesting than mine.
4. Your essay is very well written.
5. His boat must be repaired.
6. They are not pleased with the report.
7. His email explained the situation clearly.
8. The fault is completely mine.
9. We wanted to supply them with enough material for the project.
10. Our teacher reminded us about the due dates.

PRACTICE B Labeling Pronouns

Read each sentence. On the line provided, write whether the underlined pronoun is in the nominative case, the objective case, or the possessive case.

Example: Send <u>them</u> the package right away.
Answer: objective

1. The famous writer is <u>my</u> best friend. _____
2. <u>We</u> are responsible for dealing with the crisis. _____
3. The debater responded to <u>her</u> objection quickly. _____
4. The company published <u>its</u> annual report. _____
5. The doctor gave <u>her</u> the necessary medical information. _____
6. Jiang will feed and walk <u>our</u> dog today. _____
7. The librarian answered <u>their</u> questions during the meeting. _____
8. <u>She</u> is the best person for the job. _____
9. Marilyn told <u>us</u> not to worry about the decision. _____
10. The squirrel buried <u>its</u> acorns in the garden. _____

Writing and Speaking Application

Write three sentences about a school event, using nominative, objective, and possessive pronouns. Then, read them to a partner. Your partner should listen for and name the case of each pronoun. Then, switch roles with your partner.

60 THE NOMINATIVE CASE OF PRONOUNS

Use the nominative case when a pronoun is (1) the subject of a verb, (2) a predicate nominative, or (3) part of a nominative absolute.

A **predicate nominative** is a noun or a nominative pronoun that follows a linking verb, such as a form of the verb *be*, and that identifies the subject of the verb. A **nominative absolute** consists of a noun or a nominative pronoun followed by a participial phrase. This chart shows examples of the main uses of the nominative case of pronouns:

As the Subject of a Verb	He is a terrific pianist.
As a Predicate Nominative	The winners were he and they.
In a Nominative Absolute	She being the winner, the judges congratulated her.

PRACTICE A Identifying Pronouns in the Nominative Case

Read each sentence. Then circle any nominative pronouns.

Example: They repaired the car motor before the race.
Answer: (They) repaired the car motor before the race.

1. My favorite art teacher is she.
2. You must attend the meeting in place of Liu.
3. It was the best presentation made in class.
4. They are the musicians.
5. Sarah and he made the posters, and Liam and I photographed them.
6. It having been filled, I applied for another job.
7. You are the favorite candidate to win this year.
8. She and I can finish the interview by then.
9. He is a member of our committee.
10. The police officer getting a medal is he.

PRACTICE B Labeling Pronouns

Read each sentence. Then, label the underlined pronoun as subject, predicate nominative, *or part of a* nominative absolute.

Example: We won't be able to attend the dance.
Answer: subject

1. Mr. Watson and I are addressing the city council tonight. _____

2. He having researched his paper, the teacher praised his hard work. _____

3. Ven and he must be in the counselor's office this afternoon. _____

4. They are speaking at the ceremony tonight. _____

5. It won't be the first time the elevator broke down. _____

6. They and Ms. Stoner will be in charge of the meeting. _____

7. She having rehearsed for the concert, the conductor then canceled it. _____

8. The fastest runner on the team is he. _____

9. Mark, Sal, and I need help with the school newspaper. _____

10. The judge who was just appointed by the governor is she. _____

Writing and Speaking Application

Write three sentences using nominative pronouns as a subject, as a predicate nominative, or as part of a nominative absolute. Then, read them to a partner. Ask your partner to identify the nominative pronouns and explain how they are used in the sentences.

Name _____ Date _____

61 THE OBJECTIVE CASE OF PRONOUNS

Use the objective case when a pronoun is (1) the direct object of a verb or of a verbal (such as an infinitive, a participle, or a gerund), (2) the indirect object of a verb or of a verbal, or (3) the object of a preposition.

This chart shows examples of the main uses of the objective case of pronouns:

Direct Object of a Verb	The employer hired him.
Direct Object of a Verbal	If they are going to the beach, I'd be happy to meet them. (*To meet* is an infinitive.)
Indirect Object of a Verb	Friends sent her a birthday present.
Indirect Object of a Verbal	Sending her the notes would be helpful. (*Sending* is a gerund.)
Object of a Preposition	Don't wave that branch above him.

PRACTICE A Identifying Objective Pronouns

Read each sentence. Then, circle the objective pronoun.

Example: Jose asked them a series of polite questions.
Answer: Jose asked (them) a series of polite questions.

1. The dog walked between us.
2. You should tell him the correct information.
3. Sanjay mailed her a birthday gift.
4. The lawyer opted to advise her against testifying in court.
5. The teacher expected better results from them.
6. The car accident did not injure him.
7. My mother waved to me.
8. The startled deer ran away from them.
9. Seeing me made my parents happy.
10. Greeting us warmly, the concierge confirmed our reservation.

PRACTICE B Labeling Objective Pronouns

Read each sentence. Then, identify the underlined objective pronoun as a direct object, an indirect object, or an object of a preposition.

Example: We drove her to the hospital.
Answer: direct object

1. Jim gave her a book. _____
2. Francisco should sit next to them in the classroom. _____
3. The loud noise startled us on the street. _____
4. The employer gave her another chance to keep the job. _____
5. Giving him the directions would be wise. _____
6. The airport official questioned us before the flight. _____
7. His friends stood in front of him after the ceremony. _____
8. A kind act would be to send him a card. _____

Writing and Speaking Application

Write a paragraph about an afterschool activity. Use at least four objective pronouns. Read your paragraph to a partner. Have your partner identify each objective pronoun. Then, switch roles with your partner.

62 THE POSSESSIVE CASE OF PRONOUNS

Use the possessive case to show ownership.

Possessive Pronouns	Example Sentences
my, mine, our, ours	This dog is <u>mine</u>. <u>Our</u> dogs seem to like each other.
your, yours	<u>Your</u> suggestion is terrific. Was the idea <u>yours</u>?
its, his, her, hers, their, theirs	<u>His</u> decision is incorrect. <u>Theirs</u> seems more practical.

Do not confuse possessive pronouns with contractions that sound the same.

Contractions: <u>You're</u> the one who should judge the contest. <u>It's</u> about to begin.

Possessive Pronouns: The teacher will answer <u>your</u> question now. You will have <u>its</u> answer soon.

PRACTICE A Identifying Possessive Pronouns

Read each sentence. Then, circle the possessive pronoun or pronouns.

Example: Her new coat is ruined.

Answer: (Her) new coat is ruined.

1. Their complaints were taken seriously.
2. I liked his review of the movie.
3. Our vacation begins in two weeks.
4. The students applauded their teacher.
5. The colt galloped to its mother.

6. The problem that must be solved is ours.
7. The packages we received are theirs.
8. The beaver gathered material for its lodge.
9. Should we meet at your house or mine?
10. My scholarship helps me go to school.

PRACTICE B Recognizing Possessive Pronouns

From the choices in parentheses, write the correct possessive pronoun to complete each sentence.

Example: Dan talked about (him, his) summer experiences in class.

Answer: his

1. (Our, Us) school team won the tournament. _____

2. Should I bring (your, you're) costume to the theater? _____

3. Should I revise (mine, my) résumé before the interview? _____

4. The company answered (its, it's) critics honestly. _____

5. The plan to reorganize the class committee is (her, hers). _____

6. I broke (my, mine) leg while skateboarding in the park. _____

7. The children jumped into (their, theirs) parents' arms. _____

8. (They're, Their) reasons for moving don't make sense to me. _____

9. (Our, Ours) trip will include a visit to the beach. _____

10. Jeremy wanted (him, his) photograph to be in the yearbook. _____

Writing and Speaking Application

Write a paragraph about a place you'd like to visit. Use at least five possessive pronouns. Read your paragraph to a partner. Have your partner identify the possessive pronouns. Then, switch roles with your partner.

63 USING *WHO* AND *WHOM* CORRECTLY

Who is used for the nominative case. Whom is used for the objective case.

When *who* and *whom* are used as interrogative pronouns in questions, they follow rules similar to the rules for personal pronouns: Use the nominative case (*who*) for the subject of a verb or for a predicate nominative. Use the objective case (*whom*) for a direct object, for an indirect object, or for the object of a preposition.

When *who* or *whom* introduces a subordinate clause, such as a relative clause or a noun clause, its form depends on its role in the subordinate clause. If it is the subject of the verb in the subordinate clause, use the nominative case (*who*). If it is the direct or indirect object of the verb in the subordinate clause, use the objective case (*whom*).

Case	Pronouns	Use in Sentences
Nominative	who (*or* whoever)	**Who** answered the ad? (subject) The speaker is **who**? (predicate nominative) We weren't sure **who** would drive. (subject of the subordinate clause)
Objective	whom (*or* whomever)	**Whom** will you be calling? (direct object) To **whom** are we sending the card? (object of the preposition) We knew **whom** the caller wanted. (direct object of the subordinate clause)

PRACTICE A Identifying Interrogative and Relative Pronouns
Underline the interrogative or relative pronoun in each sentence.

Example: With whom are you planning the party?
Answer: With <u>whom</u> are you planning the party?

1. Whoever requested this will get a copy.
2. To whom did Sheila complain about the noise?
3. We weren't sure who yelled.
4. With whom is Yoshiro traveling this summer?
5. Give this book to whomever you choose.
6. Who will attend the ceremony with Carolina?
7. Whom should I question about the report?
8. She is a performer who is always remarkable to see.
9. Whoever wrote this report, please get in touch with me.
10. The winner of the award is who?

PRACTICE B Labeling Interrogative and Relative Pronouns
Read each sentence. Then, on the line provided, write whether each underlined pronoun is in the nominative *case or the* objective *case.*

Example: <u>Who</u> will be our candidate in the election?
Answer: <u>nominative</u>

1. Everyone knows <u>who</u> the best writer on the newspaper is. _____

2. To <u>whom</u> did you send an email about the event we planned? _____

3. With <u>whom</u> did you attend the concert? _____

4. <u>Whom</u> should we thank for preparing this meal? _____

5. Please answer <u>whoever</u> asked the question from the audience. _____

6. <u>Who</u> addressed this package to the wrong customer? _____

Writing and Speaking Application
Write four sentences about a group project in your class. Use at least three examples of *who* and *whom*. Then, read your sentences to a partner. Your partner should tell whether you used *who* and *whom* correctly. Then, switch roles with your partner.

64 PRONOUNS IN ELLIPTICAL CLAUSES

An elliptical clause is one in which some words are left out but are still understood.

In elliptical clauses beginning with *than* or *as*, use the form of the pronoun that you would use if the clause were fully stated. To determine the case, mentally add the missing words.

Objective Case: If the missing words come *before* the pronoun, choose the objective case.

> The noise bothered Yoshiro more than **me**.
> The noise bothered Yoshiro more than [the noise bothered] me.

Nominative Case: If the missing words come *after* the pronoun, choose the nominative case.

> Gabriela enjoyed the play as much as **I**.
> Gabriela enjoyed the play as much as I [enjoyed the play].

PRACTICE A Identifying Elliptical Clauses

Read each sentence. Underline the elliptical clause.

Example: Sally is as talented as I.
Answer: Sally is as talented <u>as I</u>.

1. You complained to Ron more than me.
2. She is as committed to the cause as I.
3. Miguel likes going to movies more than I.
4. Beatriz called John more than me.
5. Mom is more worried about it than I.

6. Josh goes swimming with Fran more than me.
7. Tad worked with Ellen more than me.
8. Cleo is as experienced a writer as she.
9. Lonnie encouraged Fernando more than me.
10. Chen wanted the puppy more than I.

PRACTICE B Labeling Pronouns in Elliptical Clauses

Read each sentence. Circle the pronoun in the elliptical clause. Then, label the case of the pronoun as nominative *or* objective.

Example: Mia plays the piano more than I.
Answer: Mia plays the piano more than Ⓘ. <u>nominative</u>

1. Len's sister enjoys running more than he. _____

2. Sarah is more interested in seeing the movie than she. _____

3. I am not as pleased with the group report as she. _____

4. You shared more of your art supplies with Hakim than me. _____

5. Rene is better organized than I. _____

6. Hannah spent more time with Omari than me. _____

7. That runner is as tired as I. _____

8. Julio helped Thomas more than me. _____

Writing and Speaking Application

Write a paragraph in which you use three elliptical clauses. Read the paragraph to a partner. Have your partner identify the elliptical clauses. Then, switch roles with your partner.

65 NUMBER IN NOUNS, PRONOUNS, AND VERBS

Number shows whether a noun, a pronoun, or a verb is singular or plural.

- Most nouns form their plurals by adding -s or -es. Some, such as *tooth* and *woman*, form the plurals irregularly: *teeth*, *women*.

- This chart shows the different forms of personal pronouns used as subjects.

	Always Singular	Singular or Plural	Always Plural
First Person	I		we
Second Person		you	
Third Person	it, she, he	they	

- A verb form will always be singular if it has had an -s or -es added to it or it includes the words *has*, *am*, *is*, or *was*. The number of any other verb depends on its subject.

- This chart shows verb forms that are always singular and those than can be singular or plural.

Verbs That Are Always Singular		Verbs That Can Be Singular or Plural	
(it, she, he) walks (it, she, he) has	(I) am (it, she, he) is (I, it, she, he) was	(I, we, you, they) walk (I, we, you, they) have	(we, you, they) are (we, you, they) were

PRACTICE A Identifying Number in Nouns, Pronouns, and Verbs

Read each word. Then, write whether the word is singular, plural, *or* both.

Example: dictionaries
Answer: plural

1. mice _____
2. oxen _____
3. were _____
4. has _____

5. discovery _____
6. we _____
7. have _____
8. is _____

PRACTICE B Labeling Nouns, Verbs, and Pronouns

Read each sentence. Label the underlined word as singular *or* plural. *(Consider how the word is used in the sentence.)*

Example: They <u>have</u> practiced every day.
Answer: plural

1. We <u>have</u> studied about that artist in class. _____
2. Billy <u>was</u> concerned about his sick dog. _____
3. I <u>am</u> sending you my application form today. _____
4. Many volunteers <u>were</u> involved in solving the mystery. _____
5. All the <u>children</u> were swimming in the community pool. _____
6. He <u>jumps</u> on the trampoline in gym class. _____

Writing and Speaking Application

Write three sentences in which you use singular and plural nouns, verbs, and pronouns. Read your sentences to a partner. Your partner should identify the singular and plural nouns, verbs, and pronouns. Then, switch roles with your partner.

Name _____ Date _____

66 SINGULAR AND PLURAL SUBJECTS

A singular subject must have a singular verb. A plural subject must have a plural verb.

See the examples below.

Singular Subject and Verb	Plural Subject and Verb
The **scientist works** in the lab.	The **scientists work** in the lab.
Zoe is looking for her dog.	Zoe's **parents are looking** for their dog.
Beth was cleaning her room.	The **sisters were cleaning** their room.
The **bank has closed** that branch.	The **banks have closed** those branches.

PRACTICE A Identifying Singular and Plural Subjects

Read each sentence. Circle the subject. If the subject is singular, write S. *If the subject is plural, write* P.

Example: The writer is always working.
Answer: The ⟨writer⟩ is always working. S

1. Wild elephants stampede across the plains. _____

2. The campers were not happy about the long hike in the park. _____

3. The local newspaper is offering internships this summer. _____

4. The community leaders have complained about the new law. _____

5. Those oxen were transferred to a farm last week. _____

6. Asia is the site of many early civilizations. _____

7. I am nominating Eva as class president. _____

8. Those gems are very valuable. _____

PRACTICE B Identifying Singular and Plural Subjects and Verbs

Read each sentence. Then, rewrite the sentence, underlining the subject and using the correct form of the verb in parentheses.

Example: They (is, are) moving on Saturday.
Answer: <u>They</u> are moving on Saturday.

1. My sister (live, lives) in the Pacific Northwest.

_____

2. Rangers (has, have) posted warnings about leaving campfires unattended.

_____

3. Several students (was, were) planning a surprise party for Ms. Khan.

_____

4. All summer, the geologist (has, have) been studying the rocks in that area.

_____

Writing and Speaking Application

Write three sentences about your favorite movie. Use correct singular and plural subject-verb agreement in your sentences. Read your sentences to a partner. Have your partner identify the singular and plural nouns and verbs. Then, switch roles with your partner.

67 COMPOUND SUBJECTS

A compound subject has two or more simple subjects, which are usually joined by *or, nor,* or *and*.

- A compound subject joined by *and* is generally plural and must have a plural verb.

  Two Singular Subjects: The **school** and a **playground have** opened.
  Two Plural Subjects: **Schools** and **playgrounds have** opened.
  Singular Subject and Plural Subject: Two **schools** and a **playground have** opened.

- Two or more singular subjects joined by *or* or *nor* must have a singular verb.

  Snow or **sleet is** expected this weekend.

- Two or more plural subjects joined by *or* or *nor* must have a plural verb.

  Neither the **mayors** nor the **governors are** attending the conference.

- If a singular subject is joined to a plural subject by *or* or *nor*, the subject closest to the verb determines agreement.

  Neither the **musician** nor his **fans look** pleased.
  Neither the **fans** nor the **musician looks** pleased.

PRACTICE A Identifying Compound Subjects

Read each sentence. Underline the simple subjects that form the compound subject in the sentence.

Example: The strawberries and plums are used to make jam.
Answer: The <u>strawberries</u> and <u>plums</u> are used to make jam.

1. The sea and the sky were gray.
2. The musicians and their instruments have arrived safely.
3. Either a dog or several puppies are featured in the commercial.
4. Neither the washing machines nor the television is out of order today.
5. Salads and fresh berries have been added to the cafeteria menu.
6. Frogs or toads live in that pond.
7. A light or a beacon is flickering in the distance.
8. Both the chairs and the tables were sold at the auction.
9. Her essays and novel are being published next year.
10. Neither the library nor the gym is hiring new workers.

PRACTICE B Recognizing Correct Verb Forms

Read each sentence. Circle the form of the verb that agrees with the compound subject.

Example: The cod and the salmon (is, are) fresh today.
Answer: The cod and the salmon (is, are) fresh today.

1. The historic building and the museums (is, are) highlights of the trip.
2. Neither the reporter nor the photographers (has, have) worked here before.
3. A sophomore or a junior (is, are) right for that role.
4. John and Maria (practice, practices) in the gym every weekend.
5. Anna and her sisters often (visit, visits) this store during their vacation.
6. The beach chair and towel (is, are) full of sand.

Writing and Speaking Application

Write three sentences in which you include compound subjects. Read your sentences to a partner. Your partner should identify the compound subjects and the verbs in your sentences. Then, switch roles with your partner.

Name _____ Date _____

68 CONFUSING SUBJECTS

A verb must agree in number with its subject. In some sentences, the subject comes after the verb. To find out which verb form is correct, mentally rearrange the sentence into subject-verb order.

EXAMPLE: In the pond **are** many beautiful **fish**.   REARRANGED: Many beautiful **fish are** in the pond.
EXAMPLE: Where **are** my **friends**?   REARRANGED: My **friends are** where?

The words *there* and *here* often signal an inverted sentence. They never act as the subject of a sentence.

EXAMPLES: Here **is** the **package** you ordered.   There **are** warm **blankets** in the closet.

PRACTICE A Identifying Singular and Plural Subjects

Read each sentence. Circle the subject. Then, write S if the subject is singular or P if it is plural.

Example: Here are the new books.
Answer: Here are the new (books). P

1. Near the road is a winding path. _____
2. There is the map for the trip. _____
3. Who are the people in the auditorium? _____
4. There is the new monitor. _____

5. Why are the babies still crying? _____
6. At the top of the tree is the bird's nest. _____
7. Behind the barn is the pasture. _____
8. Where are the best restaurants in town? _____

PRACTICE B Recognizing Correct Verb Forms

Read each sentence. Rewrite it with the correct form of the verb in parentheses.

Example: Who (is, are) the players in the starting lineup?
Answer: Who are the players in the starting lineup?

1. There (is, are) a list of historic sites in the region.

_____

2. Behind the school parking lot (is, are) the storage area.

_____

3. Why (was, were) the abandoned cars left here?

_____

4. Under the bed (was, were) the art supplies I had misplaced.

_____

5. Here (is, are) old books you need for the report.

_____

Writing and Speaking Application

Use sentences 1 and 2 in Practice B as models to write similar sentences. Read the sentences to a partner. Your partner should complete each sentence with the form of the verb that agrees with the subject. Then, switch roles with your partner.

69 AGREEMENT BETWEEN PRONOUNS AND ANTECEDENTS

An antecedent is the word or group of words that a pronoun stands in for. In general, a personal or possessive pronoun must agree with its antecedent in person, number, and **gender**.

EXAMPLES: **John** stored **his** luggage in the locker.
The **students** were surprised by **their** test results.

- Use a singular pronoun (a form of *I, you, it, she, he,* or *they*) when two or more singular antecedents are joined by *or* or *nor*.

    Neither **Sarah** <u>nor</u> **Mary** will talk to **her** brother.

- Use a plural pronoun (a form of *we, you,* or *they*) when two or more antecedents are joined by *and*.

    Mike's **brother** <u>and</u> **sister** brought **their** dog to the park.

- Use a plural pronoun (a form of *we, you,* or *they*) if any part of a compound antecedent joined by *or* or *nor* is plural.

    Either the **police officers** <u>or</u> the **witness** should give **their** testimony.

PRACTICE A Identifying Personal and Possessive Pronouns

For each sentence, circle the antecedent or antecedents, and underline the personal or possessive pronoun that agrees with the antecedent(s).

Example: The boy lost his way in the new school.
Answer: The (boy) lost <u>his</u> way in the new school.

1. Neither Bill nor Sal had his assignment.
2. Ms. Jenkins always returns her library books on time.
3. The dog barked at its owner in the store.
4. Neither the reporter nor the candidates had their statements ready.
5. My mother and father offered their help.
6. Wes and Dave misread their map.
7. Either the director or the actors will discuss their last interview.
8. The band was famous before it broke up.
9. The customers enjoyed their food in the newly opened restaurant.
10. The volunteers were thanked for their work.

PRACTICE B Choosing the Correct Personal or Possessive Pronoun

Read each sentence. On the line provided, write the personal or possessive pronoun in parentheses that agrees with the antecedent(s).

Example: My sister lost (her, its) invitation to the party.
Answer: <u>her</u>

1. Either my younger brother or my older brother will open (his, their) present first. _____
2. Beth will talk about (her, its) photograph in class. _____
3. The patients presented (her, their) insurance cards to the receptionist. _____
4. Our school has a flagpole on (its, their) roof. _____
5. The mayor praised the teachers for (her, their) work. _____
6. The wrestler and his opponent both fought (his, their) hardest. _____

Writing and Speaking Application

Write three sentences in which you use personal pronouns that agree with their antecedents. Read your sentences to a partner. Your partner should identify each personal pronoun and its antecedent. Then, switch roles with your partner.

Name _____ Date _____

70 AGREEMENT WITH INDEFINITE PRONOUNS

When the antecedent of a personal or possessive pronoun is an indefinite pronoun, the pronouns must agree.

Some indefinite pronouns are always singular, some are always plural, and some may be either singular or plural, depending on context.

Always Singular	another, anybody, anyone, anything, each, either, everybody, everyone, everything, little, much, neither, nobody, no one, nothing, one, other, somebody, someone, something
Singular or Plural	all, any, more, most, none, some
Always Plural	both, few, many, others, several

- Use a plural personal or possessive pronoun when the antecedent is a plural indefinite pronoun.

  Example: Many of the workers complemented **their** boss.

- Use a singular personal or possessive pronoun when the antecedent is a singular indefinite pronoun. (If the indefinite pronoun refers to people of only one gender, use a personal or possessive pronoun that corresponds to that gender—such as *he* or *she*. If the indefinite pronoun may refer to people of any gender, use a form of singular *they*.)

  Examples: Each of the girls will practice **her** part in the science presentation.

  Everyone attending the concert had to present **their** ticket at the door.

PRACTICE A Identifying Pronouns

Read each sentence. Underline the indefinite pronoun, and circle the personal or possessive pronoun that refers back to it.

Example: Most of the customers expressed their displeasure.

Answer: <u>Most</u> of the customers expressed (their) displeasure.

1. All of the tennis players showed their talent.
2. Some of the actors forgot their lines.
3. Both of the students displayed their projects.
4. All of the musicians cleaned their instruments.
5. Most of the dogs waited patiently for their baths.
6. One of the boys brought his dog.
7. Most of the donated food retained its freshness.
8. Each of the girls bought her own meal.
9. Some of the workers ate their lunches at picnic tables.
10. Each of the women presented her concerns to the revised tax laws.

PRACTICE B Choosing the Correct Indefinite Pronoun

Read each sentence. Underline the personal or possessive pronoun in parentheses that agrees with the indefinite pronoun.

Example: All of the teachers will talk with (his, their) students.

Answer: All of the teachers will talk with (his, <u>their</u>) students.

1. Just one of the male singers forgot (his, their) part.
2. All of the parents watched (his, their) children practice soccer.
3. Each of the grandmothers was pleased with (her, their) gifts.
4. Many of the police officers praised (their, his) new police chief.
5. All of the reporters carried (his, their) credentials.

Writing and Speaking Application

Write a short paragraph about an interesting job. Use three personal or possessive pronouns that agree with their indefinite pronoun antecedents. Read your paragraph to a partner. Your partner should identify the pronouns that agree. Then, switch roles with your partner.

71 AGREEMENT WITH REFLEXIVE AND INTENSIVE PRONOUNS

Reflexive pronouns and intensive pronouns, which both end in *-self* or *-selves*, must agree with their antecedents.

Like personal and possessive pronouns, a reflexive or intensive pronoun must agree with its antecedent. Unlike personal and possessive pronouns, a reflexive or intensive pronoun's antecedent must always appear in the same sentence as the pronoun.

EXAMPLE: **Olga** made that bookshelf **herself**. (intensive)

They helped **themselves** to the free food. (reflexive)

The **dog** found **itself** a shady spot in which to nap. (reflexive)

PRACTICE A Identifying Reflexive and Intensive Pronouns

Read each sentence. Then write the reflexive or intensive pronoun on the line provided.

Example: She will improve herself by taking that course.
Answer: herself

1. I washed the dishes myself. _____

2. The boy enjoyed himself at the game. _____

3. Isabella believed herself to be a wonderful writer. _____

4. The dog took care of itself when it was lost. _____

5. We ourselves can complete the project. _____

6. My brothers finished building the tree house themselves. _____

7. The winning team members looked at themselves and smiled. _____

PRACTICE B Identifying Pronouns and Their Antecedents

Read each sentence. Then, draw an arrow from the reflexive or intensive pronoun to its antecedent.

Example: The athlete balanced herself on the trampoline.

Answer: The athlete balanced herself on the trampoline.

1. Carlos found himself lost in as unfamiliar area.

2. The doctor looked for the test results herself.

3. The children laughed at themselves during the play.

4. The new cook showed himself to the kitchen.

5. David proved himself a success.

6. You can update the software yourself.

7. Tamara rebuilt the car motor herself.

8. The successful musician was proud of herself.

Writing and Speaking Application

Write a paragraph in which you use at least three reflexive pronouns. Then, read your paragraph to a partner. Your partner should listen for and identify each reflexive pronoun and its antecedent.

72 VAGUE PRONOUN REFERENCES

To avoid confusion, a pronoun requires an antecedent that is either stated or clearly understood.

- The pronouns *which, this, that, these,* and *those* should not be used to refer to a vague or overly general idea.

Vague Reference: The house had heating and plumbing issues. **These** concerned us.

Rewritten: The house had heating and plumbing issues. **These problems** concerned us.

- The personal pronouns *it, they,* and *you* should always have a clear antecedent.

Vague Reference: In the newspaper, **they** quoted our governor's speech.

Rewritten: In the newspaper, **two reporters** quoted our governor's speech.

PRACTICE A Identifying Vague Pronoun References

Read each sentence. Then, underline the vague pronoun.

Example: They brought their purchases back to the store.

Answer: <u>They</u> brought their purchases back to the store.

1. Brady is a nervous person, and it shows when he meets people.

2. My friends can't go swimming if they won't open the community pool.

3. Mattie won the prize, which is why she is proud.

4. At the beginning of the ceremony, they announced the award recipients.

5. You must pass certain tests to get a driver's license.

6. The bus waited in traffic, and that annoyed everyone.

7. In most comic books, these are colorful.

8. Throughout the community meeting, they were rude.

PRACTICE B Correcting Vague Pronoun References

Read each sentence. Then, rewrite the sentence in a way that corrects the use of a vague pronoun. There are multiple correct ways to do so.

Example: I don't know much about music, but they say it makes a person smarter.

Answer: <u>I don't know much about music, but experts say it makes a person smarter.</u>

1. The computers are still broken, which is frustrating.

_____

2. When the market closed, they complained to the manager.

_____

3. The chef picked produce from his garden, and these improved the dinner.

_____

4. To complete the class project, you will have to work after school this week.

_____

5. On the can, it didn't list all the ingredients.

_____

Writing and Speaking Application

Write a short review of a favorite television show. Use at least three vague pronouns. Then read your paragraph to a partner. Your partner should listen for and identify the vague references and explain how to rewrite each sentence correctly. Then, switch roles with your partner.

73 AMBIGUOUS PRONOUN REFERENCES

A pronoun is ambiguous when there is more than one antecedent to which it might refer.

Ambiguous pronouns are confusing to readers. In the sentence below, the pronoun *he* is confusing because it might refer to either *Frank* or *Sam*. Notice how repeating the antecedent, rather than using an ambiguous pronoun, makes the sentence's meaning clear.

Ambiguous: *Frank emailed Sam before **he** left school.*

Clear: *Frank emailed Sam before **Sam** left school.*

PRACTICE A Identifying Ambiguous Pronoun References

Read each sentence. On the line provided, write the ambiguous pronoun.

Example: Claire ordered a blouse from the catalogue, but it was lost.
Answer: <u>it</u>

1.   Whenever Mark meets Frank, he is always late. _____

2.   Marissa told Felicia that she had to go to the science lab. _____

3.   Jorge and Liam went to the skatepark, where he had lost a backpack. _____

4.   Whenever Kristen works with Eva, she becomes upset. _____

5.   The customer called the manager, and he was concerned. _____

6.   Amanda told Keisha that she had a meeting to get to. _____

PRACTICE B Correcting Ambiguous Pronoun References

Read each sentence. Then, rewrite the sentence in a way that corrects the use of ambiguous pronouns. There are multiple correct ways to do so.

Example: Frank talked to Drew about the new book he read last week.
Answer: <u>Frank talked to Drew about the new book Frank read last week.</u>

1.   Gabriela and Tosha discussed the software that she had uncovered.

_____

2.   When my father and Uncle Luis go camping, he always enjoys himself.

_____

3.   After Mom bought Karen a new coat, she decided to return it.

_____

4.   Miguel and Aaron made posters for the school play that he stars in.

_____

Writing and Speaking Application

Write three sentences with ambiguous pronouns. Then, read your sentences to a partner. Your partner should identify the ambiguous pronoun in each sentence and explain how to correct it. Then, switch roles with your partner.

74 AVOIDING DISTANT PRONOUN REFERENCES

A personal pronoun should always be close enough to its antecedent to prevent confusion.

You can correct a distant pronoun reference by changing the pronoun to a noun.

Distant Reference: Mr. Mullen forgot his computer at the store. He meant to go back right away, but then he got distracted by his son and a game of baseball. When he went back and looked, **it** was lost.

Corrected: Mr. Mullen forgot his computer at the store. He meant to go back right away, but then he got distracted by his son and a game of baseball. When he went back and looked, **his computer** was lost.

PRACTICE A Identifying Distant Pronoun References

Read each group of sentences. Underline the distant pronoun.

Example: Marty looked for his keys. He looked under the bed and found his shoes. He looked on his desk and found the paper that had been due yesterday. He asked his mother for help. His mother didn't know where they were either.

Answer: His mother didn't know where <u>they</u> were either.

1. The artist was working on some sketches when he decided he needed to eat lunch. He left the windows of the studio open. While he was at lunch, a storm came through and rain pelted down. They were ruined.

2. We planned our vacation carefully, but our plane was delayed, the hotel lost our reservation, and the car broke down. It was a disaster.

3. Preparing the dish was complicated. All the ingredients had to be fresh. All the fruit had to be chopped. The cream had to be whipped by hand. It took a long time to prepare.

PRACTICE B Correcting Distant Pronoun References

Read each group of sentences. Then, on the line provided, rewrite the final sentence in the group to correct a distant pronoun reference.

Example: Mia found an old bike in the garage. The bike had flat tires and some rust. Clearly, the bike had been sitting for a long time. However, she thought it could be fixed up and used.

Answer: <u>However, Mia thought it could be fixed up and used.</u>

1. The hero in the novel defeats the villain. The village rejoices and shares a feast to celebrate this hard-won victory. Then, he leaves to seek the missing treasure.

_____

2. Sal designed the colorful posters for the school dance. Then, he blew up balloons and set out some chairs. Sal plans to design them next year, too.

_____

3. The missing dog was found. All the neighbors helped to look—even Mr. Wendt, who I don't know very well. It is safe now.

_____

Writing and Speaking Application

Use items 2 and 3 in Practice A as models for writing similar examples of distant pronoun use. Then, read your sentences aloud to a partner. Your partner should identify each distant pronoun reference and explain how to correct it.

Name _____ Date _____

75 RECOGNIZING DEGREES OF COMPARISON

Modifiers (adjectives and adverbs) have three degrees of comparison—the positive, the comparative, and the superlative.

The positive degree is the base form of an adjective or an adverb. Use the comparative degree to compare <u>two</u> items. Use the superlative degree to compare <u>three</u> or more items.

Modifiers are changed to show degree in three ways: (1) by adding -er or -est, (2) by adding *more* or *most*, or (3) by using entirely different words. The following chart shows examples of adjectives and adverbs in each of the three degrees.

Adjective			Adverb		
Positive	**Comparative**	**Superlative**	**Positive**	**Comparative**	**Superlative**
cold	colder	coldest	coldly	more coldly	most coldly
bountiful	more bountiful	most bountiful	bountifully	more bountifully	most bountifully
good	better	best	well	better	best

PRACTICE A Identifying Adjectives and Adverbs

Read each sentence. Then, underline the descriptive adjective or adverb. On the line provided, write adjective *or* adverb *to identify the underlined word(s).*

Example: My sister is proud of the story she wrote.
Answer: My sister is <u>proud</u> of the story she wrote.   <u>adjective</u>

1.   They worked more diligently than the adults. _____

2.   Martha's grades are satisfactory. _____

3.   The storm blew fiercely across the plains. _____

4.   That costume for the play is the most beautiful. _____

5.   Ted acted more casually than Leo. _____

6.   The scientist talked most humbly. _____

PRACTICE B Identifying Degrees of Comparison

Read each sentence. On the line provided, identify the degree of the underlined word(s) as positive, comparative, *or* superlative.

Example: This test is the <u>hardest</u> of all.
Answer: <u>superlative</u>

1.   I think that is a <u>better</u> suggestion than the other one. _____

2.   Ed is <u>happiest</u> when he's working hard on his car. _____

3.   That dancer moved <u>most gracefully</u> across the stage. _____

4.   The bird's <u>shrill</u> cry startled us. _____

5.   Mark played basketball <u>better</u> today than yesterday. _____

Writing and Speaking Application

Write a short description of a place in your community. Use at least five examples of positive, comparative, and superlative degrees of adjectives and adverbs. Read your description to a partner. Your partner should identify the degrees of comparison. Then, switch roles with your partner.

Name _____ Date _____

76 REGULAR COMPARATIVE AND SUPERLATIVE FORMS

The number of syllables in regular modifiers determines how their degrees are formed.

- Use *-er* or *more* to form the comparative degree and *-est* or *most* to form the superlative degree of most one-and two-syllable modifiers.

	Positive	Comparative	Superlative
Examples:	clear	clearer	clearest
	wishful	more wishful	most wishful

- Use *more* and *most* to form the comparative and superlative degrees of all modifiers with three or more syllables.

  Examples: industrious   more industrious   most industrious

- All adverbs that end in *-ly* form their comparative and superlative degrees with *more* and *most*.

  Examples: silently   more silently   most silently

PRACTICE A Identifying Regular Comparative and Superlative Forms
Read each sentence. On the line provided, write C if the underlined word or words are in the comparative degree or S if the underlined word or words are in the superlative degree.

Example: That building is <u>taller</u> than this one.
Answer: <u>C</u>

1. The sailboats are moving <u>more gracefully</u> today than yesterday. _____

2. Len is the <u>most skillful</u> worker in the factory. _____

3. This new air conditioner runs <u>more quietly</u> than the old one did. _____

4. David is <u>more willing</u> to take part in class activities this year. _____

5. According to the news report, this is the <u>toughest</u> campaign ever. _____

PRACTICE B Writing Regular Comparative and Superlative Forms
Read each sentence. Then, on the line provided, write the correct form of the modifier in parentheses.

Example: That movie has the _____ special effects. (marvelous — superlative)
Answer: That movie has the <u>most marvelous</u> special effects.

1. Kendra is the _____ member of our team. (competitive — superlative)

2. That star shines _____ in the night sky. (brightly — superlative)

3. Exercising is _____ to your health than inactivity. (beneficial — comparative)

4. The days are _____ in the summer than in the fall. (long — comparative)

5. This has been the _____ summer in years. (warm — superlative)

Writing and Speaking Application
Write several sentences about your favorite TV show or movie. Use at least three regular adjectives and adverbs in the comparative and superlative degrees. Read your sentences to a partner. Your partner should identify the adjectives and adverbs in the comparative and superlative degrees. Then, switch roles with your partner.

Name _____ Date _____

77 IRREGULAR COMPARATIVE AND SUPERLATIVE FORMS

The comparative and superlative degrees of a few commonly used modifiers are formed in unpredictable ways. Therefore, the irregular comparative and superlative forms of these adjectives and adverbs must be memorized.

Positive	Comparative	Superlative
bad, badly, ill	worse	worst
far (distance) far (extent)	farther further	farthest furthest
good, well	better	best
late	later or latter	latest or last
little (amount)	less	least
many, much	more	most

PRACTICE A Identifying Irregular Comparative and Superlative Forms

Read each sentence. Underline the irregular comparative or superlative modifier.

Example: Cam is probably the best player on the team.
Answer: Cam is probably the <u>best</u> player on the team.

1. The riders rode farther today than yesterday.
2. I think this year's prom theme is better than last year's.
3. The blue bike costs more than the red one.
4. Amir's stew is made with less broth than Sheila's.
5. That candidate has offered the least evidence to support his position.
6. The new law goes further to protect animals than the old one did.
7. That was the worst meal I've eaten in weeks.
8. The farthest I've been from home was on a trip to Toronto.
9. This version of the play has the most revisions of all.
10. This translation is worse than the first.

PRACTICE B Writing Irregular Comparative and Superlative Forms

Read each sentence. On the line provided, complete the sentence with the form of the modifier indicated in parentheses.

Example: The migrating birds flew _____ today than they did yesterday. (far)
Answer: The migrating birds flew <u>farther</u> today than they did yesterday.

1. That's the _____ problem that we have to solve on this committee. (bad — superlative)
2. The park saw _____ visitors this year than last year. (many — comparative)
3. That interview is the_____ source of information about the new mayor. (good — superlative)
4. I have _____ expertise in this area than you do. (little — comparative)
5. Toni's grades have shown the _____ improvement this year. (much — superlative)

Writing and Speaking Application

Use the sentences in Practice B as models to write similar sentences. Then, read the sentences to a partner. Have your partner complete each sentence with the correct form of the modifier. Then, switch roles with your partner.

78 USING COMPARATIVE AND SUPERLATIVE DEGREES

In general, the comparative degree is used to compare <u>two</u> items, whereas the superlative degree is used to compare <u>three or more</u> items.

Comparative: That writer is **more talented** than this one.

That cartoon is **sillier** than this one.

Superlative: That writer is the **most talented** one in the group.

That cartoon is the **silliest** of all.

PRACTICE A Identifying Comparative and Superlative Degrees of Modifiers

Read each sentence. Underline the modifiers used for comparison. Then, on the line provided, write C *if the modifier is comparative or* S *if the modifier is superlative.*

Example: Dan swims slower than I do.
Answer: Dan swims <u>slower</u> than I do. C

1. Ahmed is the most experienced member of the team. _____

2. His horse gallops faster than mine. _____

3. Mia is the most practical person in the group. _____

4. Morgan is the strangest character in the novel. _____

5. Those apple trees are the tallest trees in the orchard. _____

6. This wool sweater is softer than that one. _____

7. Mr. Ramirez is the most generous contributor to the charity. _____

8. Main Street Café makes the best pizza in the city. _____

9. That is the tiniest bird in the nest. _____

10. Stan is the humblest writer in the entire class. _____

PRACTICE B Correcting Mistakes in Usage of Modifiers

Read each sentence. On the line provided, rewrite the sentence to correct the error in modifier usage.

Example: That story is most interesting than mine.
Answer: <u>That story is more interesting than mine.</u>

1. Ling is the harder worker on our team.

_____

2. She wrote most school newspaper articles than her older brother last year.

_____

3. That sofa is heaviest than this one.

_____

4. This cake is tastiest than the one Diego made last week.

_____

5. That scene was the funnier of the entire movie.

_____

Writing and Speaking Application

Write a short paragraph in which you use at least three modifiers in the comparative and superlative degrees. Read your paragraph to a partner. Your partner should listen for and identify the modifiers. Then, switch roles with your partner.

Name _____ Date _____

79 MAKING LOGICAL COMPARISONS

Your sentences should compare only items of a similar kind.

UNBALANCED: **Ellen's bike** is faster than **June**.
CORRECT: **Ellen's bike** is faster than **June's**.

UNBALANCED: The **speed of the train** is faster than the **car**.
CORRECT: The **speed of the train** is faster than the **speed of the car**.

When comparing one of a group with the rest of the group, make sure that your sentence contains the word *other* or the word *else*.

ILLOGICAL: **Chuck** was slower than **any runner**. *(Chuck cannot be slower than himself.)*
LOGICAL: **Chuck** was slower than **any other runner**.

PRACTICE A Identifying Illogical Comparisons

Read each sentence. Underline any unbalanced or illogical comparisons. If the sentence is correct as written, write C on the line.

Example: Tom is busier than any worker in the store.
Answer: Tom is busier <u>than any worker</u> in the store.

1. My typing speed is faster than Olivia. _____

2. Anna sings better than anyone in the club. _____

3. Joon's tote bag is sturdier than Leo's. _____

4. Hakim's puppy is friskier than Mike. _____

5. Cho is a better student than anyone in the class. _____

6. The sound of the bell is louder than the whistle. _____

7. The strength of the steel beam is greater than the strength of the wood beam. _____

8. That dog is friendlier than any dog in the neighborhood. _____

PRACTICE B Writing Clear Comparisons

Read each sentence. Then, on the line provided, rewrite the sentence to correct any comparison that is unbalanced or illogical.

Example: José's drawing is smaller than Ellie.
Answer: <u>José's drawing is smaller than Ellie's.</u>

1. The smell of the chocolate cake is sweeter than the apple pie.

_____

2. Our team has won more games than any team in the league.

_____

3. The success of that play is greater than the musical.

_____

4. Abdullah's poems are longer than Keiko.

_____

Writing and Speaking Application

Write several sentences in which you use comparisons that are unbalanced or illogical. Read your sentences to a partner. Your partner should listen for and identify the faulty comparisons and explain how to correct them.

80 USING ABSOLUTE MODIFIERS LOGICALLY

An absolute modifier is an adjective or an adverb whose meaning is entirely contained in the positive degree. Avoid using absolute modifiers illogically.

Some common absolute modifiers are *dead, entirely, fatal, final, identical, infinite, opposite, perfect, right, straight, wrong,* and *unique.*

Avoid using adverbs to modify absolute modifiers. For example, a decision can be *final,* but it cannot be *completely final.* Similarly, avoid using the comparative and superlative forms of absolute modifiers. For example, an idea can be *unique,* but it cannot be *more unique* than another idea.

> **Incorrect:** That painting looks **perfectly straight** on the wall.
>
> **Correct:** That painting looks **straight** on the wall.

PRACTICE A Identifying Illogical Use of Absolute Modifiers

Read each sentence. Underline the illogical use of an absolute modifier.

Example: Hector's request for dinner was the complete opposite of mine.

Answer: Hector's request for dinner was the <u>complete opposite</u> of mine.

1. The directions were entirely wrong.

2. That fashion look is most unique.

3. The two paintings look wholly identical.

4. The story turned out to be totally true.

5. My new class schedule is absolutely final.

6. This pasta tastes very perfect.

7. All living things are perfectly mortal.

8. Keira's most ultimate goal is becoming a chess champion.

9. The house plant is completely dead.

10. The scientist's theory was proved totally correct.

PRACTICE B Correcting Illogical Use of Absolute Modifiers

Read each sentence. On the line provided, rewrite the sentence to correct the illogical use of an absolute modifier.

Example: That writer's opinion is perfectly wrong.

Answer: <u>That writer's opinion is wrong.</u>

1. I think you're extremely wrong about that issue.

_____

2. David drew a most unique cover for the brochure.

_____

3. The careless driver totally missed the highway exit.

_____

4. I think the new sofa looks most wrong in that corner of the room.

_____

5. The runner completed an absolutely perfect race and won first prize.

_____

Writing and Speaking Application

Write a paragraph in which you include comparisons that illogically use absolute modifiers. Read your paragraph to a partner, who should correct the illogical uses of absolute modifiers. Then, switch roles.

Name _____ Date _____

81 RECOGNIZING DOUBLE NEGATIVES

Using two negative words in a sentence when one is sufficient is called a *double negative*. Do not use double negatives in formal writing.

Study the examples of double negatives and two different ways to correct them in the following chart:

Double Negative	Corrections
We **don't** have **no** time to waste.	We don't have any time to waste. We have no time to waste.
She **didn't** have **nothing** to do.	She didn't have anything to do. She had nothing to do.

If a sentence has more than one clause, each clause may correctly contain one negative word.

Example: *We **didn't** make it to the beach, but we **weren't** sad about it.*

PRACTICE A Identifying Double Negatives

Read each sentence. Then, underline both parts of the double negative.

Example: The mechanic didn't repair no cars.
Answer: The mechanic <u>didn't</u> repair <u>no</u> cars.

1. They haven't received no help yet.
2. Zoe doesn't have no time for video games.
3. They didn't follow no directions.
4. Mr. Abbas didn't want no reward.
5. The close friends didn't have no fight.
6. The volunteer didn't ask for nothing.
7. He doesn't never forget school assignments.
8. The hotel isn't nowhere on this map.
9. The recipe didn't require no eggs.
10. I don't think nobody agrees with that.

PRACTICE B Revising Sentences to Correct Double Negatives

Read each sentence. Then, on the line provided, rewrite the sentence to correct the double negative.

Example: I haven't got no time to study for the exam.
Answer: <u>I haven't got any time to study for the exam.</u>

1. The tired hikers didn't have no water left.

_____

2. The store manager hasn't no reason to refuse his employee's request.

_____

3. The delivery driver can't bring none of the supplies you wanted.

_____

4. The photographer never had no trouble with her camera before.

_____

5. The villagers hadn't no warning about the disastrous flood.

_____

Writing and Speaking Application

Using sentences 1, 3, 5, and 8 in Practice A as models, write four sentences with double negatives. Read your sentences to a partner. Your partner should listen for and suggest ways to correct the double negatives. Then, switch roles with your partner.

82 FORMING NEGATIVE SENTENCES CORRECTLY

The most common ways to make a statement negative are to use one negative word, such as *never, no,* or *none,* or to add the word *not* (or the contraction *-n't*) after a helping verb.

- Use only one negative word in each clause in a sentence.

  Double Negative: They **didn't** have **no** fun at the school party.

  Preferred: They **didn't** have fun at the school party.
  They had **no** fun at the school party.

- When *but* means "only," it is usually a negative. Don't use it with another negative word.

  Double Negative: There **wasn't but** one correct answer.

  Preferred: There was **but** one correct answer.
  There was **only** one correct answer.

- Do not use the words *barely, hardly,* or *scarcely* with another negative word.

  Double Negative: We **didn't** have **scarcely** enough time to finish the test.

  Preferred: We had **scarcely** enough time to finish the test.
  We **didn't** have enough time to finish the test.

PRACTICE A Identifying Double Negatives

Read each sentence. Underline the words that create a double negative.

Example: There wasn't hardly enough water in the lake.
Answer: There <u>wasn't hardly</u> enough water in the lake.

1. They hadn't but one route to travel across the mountains.

2. The run-down building hadn't hardly two windows left.

3. The teacher never had no complaints about her students.

4. The young children weren't scarcely able to reach the seats of the swings.

5. The detective never had no strong clues to solve the crime.

PRACTICE B Revising Sentences to Avoid Double Negatives

Read each sentence. On the line provided, rewrite the sentence to correct the double negative.

Example: The students hadn't but two days left before final exams.
Answer: <u>The students had two days left before final exams.</u>

1. The swimmers hadn't barely enough room in the crowded pool.

_____

2. Omar and Isabella don't have no plans for the weekend.

_____

3. The audience couldn't hardly hear a word the actors said.

_____

Writing and Speaking Application

Write a short description of an imaginary scene, using at least three double negatives. Then, read your description to a partner. Your partner should identify the double negatives and suggest how to correct them. Then, switch roles with your partner.

83 USING NEGATIVES TO CREATE UNDERSTATEMENT

Writers use understatement to express an idea indirectly—either to minimize the importance of the idea or to draw attention to it. Understatement can be achieved by using a negative word and a word with a negative prefix, such as *un-, in-, im-, dis-*, or *under-*.

Look at the following examples that use negative words to create understatement:

- They were **not uninterested** in the plot.
- We were **scarcely unconcerned** about the problem.

PRACTICE A Identifying Understatement

Read each sentence. Then, underline the words that create understatement.

Example: We did not dislike the director's new movie.
Answer: We did <u>not dislike</u> the director's new movie.

1. Her editorial isn't completely uninteresting.

2. We didn't find his excuse totally unbelievable.

3. Her intentions weren't misunderstood by the others.

4. The candidate's motives didn't go unrecognized.

5. The scientists' research wasn't considered unimportant.

6. The students' contributions weren't unappreciated by the faculty.

7. The fans' reaction to the pop star wasn't understated by any means.

8. Going on vacation this year isn't unthinkable.

PRACTICE B Using Negatives to Create Understatement

Read each sentence. Then, on the line provided, rewrite the sentence, using a negative word and a negative prefix to create understatement.

Example: Her answer is important.
Answer: <u>Her answer is not unimportant.</u>

1. We are hopeful about increasing the city budget for next year.

_____

2. The chef's hard work was appreciated by the diners.

_____

3. I estimated the difficulty of this assignment.

_____

4. The students understood the teacher's directions for taking the test.

_____

5. Matt was apologetic for forgetting to mow the lawn.

_____

Writing and Speaking Application

Write a paragraph in which you use at least three understatements. Read your paragraph to a partner. Your partner should listen for and identify the understatements. Then, switch roles with your partner.

84 COMMON USAGE PROBLEMS

A good writer masters how to avoid common usage problems, such as the ones below.

- **Ain't:** In formal writing, always use *am not, is not,* or *are not.* Never use *ain't.*

  Incorrect: He **ain't** going to the auditorium.　　Correct: He **is not** going to the auditorium.

- **Among, between:** Use *among* to show a connection among <u>three or more</u> items. Use *between* to show a connection between <u>two</u> items.

  Examples: The teacher divided the books **among** all the classes.
  　　　　　 I will ride my bike **between** those two towns.

- **Farther, further:** Use *farther* to refer to distance. Use *further* to mean "additional" or "to a greater degree."

  Examples: He must run **farther** to win the race.　　We must talk **further** about the problem.

- **Fewer, less:** Use the word *fewer* with nouns that can be counted. Use the word *less* with qualities and quantities that cannot be counted.

  Example:　**Fewer** flights would mean **less** congestion at the airport.

PRACTICE A Recognizing Usage Problems

Read each sentence. Then, circle the correct item in the parentheses to complete the sentence.

Example: If we don't hurry, we (ain't / are not) going to make it to the bus stop in time.
Answer:　If we don't hurry, we (ain't / (are not)) going to make it to the bus stop in time.

1. That (ain't, is not) the correct answer to the question.

2. We must drive much (farther, further) along this highway before dark.

3. (Fewer, Less) cars on the road would reduce traffic.

4. Felicia and Ahmed split the check (among, between) themselves.

5. I think it would be useful to examine the lab results (farther, further).

PRACTICE B Revising Sentences to Correct Usage Problems

Read each sentence. Then, on the line provided, rewrite the sentence to correct an error in usage.

Example: The children ain't going to the playground this afternoon.
Answer:　<u>The children are not going to the playground this afternoon.</u>

1. The scientist will do farther research. _____

2. They ain't growing a garden this year. _____

3. You need a space among the two words. _____

4. The petition circulated between the 75 group members. _____

5. Less ingredients made the salad tastier. _____

Writing and Speaking Application

Write a paragraph about an artist or a musician you would like to interview. In your writing, include several usage errors. Read your paragraph to a partner. Your partner should identify the usage problems and suggest corrections. Then, switch roles with your partner.

85 USING CAPITALS FOR FIRST WORDS

- Capitalize the first word in declarative, interrogative, imperative, and exclamatory sentences.

  Declarative: Our track team won the competition.
  Interrogative: Who will write this article?
  Imperative: Turn off the lights.
  Exclamatory: What a terrific idea you had!

- Capitalize the first word in interjections and incomplete questions.

  Interjections: Amazing! Wow!   **Incomplete Questions:** Where? What name?

- The word *I* is always capitalized, whether it is the first word in a sentence or not.

  Example: Mark and **I** are the co-chairs.

PRACTICE A Capitalizing Words

Read each item. Then, circle the lowercase word or words that should be capitalized.

Example: planning the class trip is fun.
Answer: (planning) the class trip is fun.

1. wow! what a time!
2. who will schedule the next meeting?
3. don't park there.
4. that's an amazing movie!
5. watch out for the icy sidewalk!

6. i think i left my notebook on the bus.
7. how many people will be at the picnic?
8. great! amazing!
9. why not? who?
10. the recycling center is open seven days a week.

PRACTICE B Rewriting Sentences With Correct Capitalization

Read each item. Then, on the line provided, rewrite the item with correct capitalization.

Example: fred volunteered to train the dog for the show.
Answer: Fred volunteered to train the dog for the show.

1. after reviewing his speech, i decided to rewrite it.

   _____

2. what a terrific plan for the community art show!

   _____

3. how many students will be able to attend the special assembly?

   _____

4. our goal is to raise more money for the new school library.

   _____

5. what? you mean we still don't have a room for the next meeting?

   _____

Writing and Speaking Application

Write a short paragraph in which you use correct capitalization. Then, read your paragraph to a partner. Your partner should identify the words that should be capitalized. Then, switch roles with your partner.

86 USING CAPITALS WITH QUOTATIONS

- Capitalize the first word of a quotation.

  Example: My brother said, "**D**on't forget Mom's birthday."

- Do <u>not</u> capitalize the first word of a continuing sentence when a quotation is interrupted by identifying words.

  Example: "After we saw you," Kwan said, "**w**e felt better."

- Do <u>not</u> capitalize the first word of a continuing sentence when the first word of a quotation is the continuation of a speaker's sentence.

  Example: Mr. Mehta said that the student project was "**a** wonderful effort."

PRACTICE A Identifying Words to Capitalize in Quotations

Read each sentence. Circle the word or words that need to be capitalized. If the sentence is correct, write correct.

Example: My friend said, "what time is the baseball game?"
Answer: My friend said, "(what) time is the baseball game?"

1. The guide said, "this museum was founded in 1895." _____

2. My grandmother said that she was thrilled "by this wonderful gift." _____

3. "when the train came into the station," he said, "everyone got on board." _____

4. Henry added, "those plants must be watered first." _____

5. "after the snow stops," Dad told us, "you can sled until dinner." _____

PRACTICE B Revising Sentences to Capitalize Quotations Correctly

Read each sentence. Then, on the line provided, rewrite the sentence to fix errors in capitalization.

Example: The vet said, "please give your dog one pill per day."
Answer: <u>The vet said, "Please give your dog one pill per day."</u>

1. "when we visited the museum," she said, "The exhibits amazed us."

    _____

2. I remarked, "let's appoint Alex the new editor of the school paper."

    _____

3. Our teacher advised, "you should write for at least one hour each day."

    _____

4. Lydia remarked that she was pleased by "This astounding attendance."

    _____

5. "during the horrible storm," Mai said, "Everyone was terrified."

    _____

Writing and Speaking Application

Write a dialogue between two imaginary characters. Read your dialogue with a partner to make sure that you used capitals with quotations correctly. Then, switch roles with your partner.

87 USING CAPITALS FOR PROPER NOUNS

Proper nouns name specific examples of people, places, or things and should be capitalized.

- Capitalize each part of a person's name—even when the full name is not used.

  Examples: Olivia Chen   A. E. Harding   Luis Gonzalez

- Capitalize geographical and place names. See the examples in the chart below.

Streets: Main Street	**Mountains:** Bear Mountain
Towns and Cities: Chicago, Boston	**Sections of a Country:** the Midwest
Counties and States: Kingston County, Maine	**Bodies of Water:** Lake Mead
Nations and Continents: Ireland, Africa	**Monuments and Memorials:** Vietnam Memorial

- Capitalize words indicating direction only when they name a specific place.

  Examples: The class report is about the **Pacific Northwest.**   The bus turns **east** here.

- Capitalize the names of specific dates, events, documents, holidays, religious holidays, periods in history, and historical events. (Do <u>not</u> capitalize articles, conjunctions, or prepositions.)

  Examples: Tuesday, October 4   the **Bill** of **Rights**   **Arbor Day**   the **Korean War**

PRACTICE A Identifying Proper Nouns

Read each sentence. Then, underline the proper noun or nouns in the sentence.

Example: We'll reach Lake Ontario on Saturday.
Answer: We'll reach <u>Lake Ontario</u> on <u>Saturday</u>.

1. Who attended the Constitutional Convention in Philadelphia?

2. Her cabin is in the foothills of the Rocky Mountains.

3. That map shows all the major rivers in Africa, Asia, and Europe.

4. Let's drive south along Waverly Place until we reach Second Avenue.

5. The judges selected the winner of the Spring Music Show on Friday.

PRACTICE B Capitalizing Proper Nouns

Read each sentence. Then, on the line provided, rewrite the sentence, capitalizing all proper nouns.

Example: My cousins will see the lincoln memorial in washington, d.c.
Answer: <u>My cousins will see the Lincoln Memorial in Washington, D.C.</u>

1. Our family is planning a trip to the grand canyon. _____

2. lisa k. smith wrote about her trip to scotland and ireland. _____

3. American troops suffered greatly at valley forge near philadelphia, pennsylvania. _____

4. The deepest lake in the united states is crater lake in oregon. _____

5. The rio grande and the st. lawrence river are in north america. _____

Writing and Speaking Application

Write a short paragraph in which you use four proper nouns. Then, read your paragraph to a partner. Your partner should identify the proper nouns that should be capitalized. Then, switch roles with your partner.

88 USING CAPITALS FOR PROPER ADJECTIVES

A proper adjective is either an adjective formed from a proper noun or a proper noun used as an adjective.

- Capitalize most proper adjectives and proper nouns used as adjectives: *Mayan temple; the Jefferson papers.*

- Capitalize a brand name when it is used as an adjective, but do not capitalize the common noun it modifies: *Work Hard sweatshirts.*

- Do <u>not</u> capitalize a common noun used with two proper adjectives: *Park and Madison avenues.*

PRACTICE A Identifying Proper Adjectives

Read each sentence. Then, circle the proper adjective.

Example: He is a famous Austrian artist.
Answer: He is a famous (Austrian) artist.

1. The Harrison house is for sale now.

2. New York cheesecake is world famous.

3. My new dog is an Italian breed.

4. That exhibit of Venetian art is closing.

5. She is a well-known Jane Austen scholar.

6. The Val Tech laptop was just released.

7. The Boston area is densely populated.

8. We went to the Brazilian festival.

9. New World plants include tomatoes and potatoes.

10. That Stay Cool refrigerator fits in our kitchen.

PRACTICE B Capitalizing Proper Adjectives

Read each sentence. Then, on the line provided, rewrite the sentence, capitalizing all proper adjectives.

Example: Simon wants to see that exhibit of american and canadian art.
Answer: Simon wants to see that exhibit of American and Canadian art.

1. The mediterranean and caribbean seas both played important roles in world history.

_____

2. american patriots got help from their french supporters in their struggle against british rule.

_____

3. The scholar will lecture about aztec architecture and egyptian mummies.

_____

4. In her book about asian cuisine, she included recipes for japanese food.

_____

5. The smithfield building is at the corner of main and elm streets.

_____

Writing and Speaking Application

Write a short paragraph about a current event. Use at least four proper adjectives. Then, read your paragraph to a partner. Your partner should identify the proper adjectives that should be capitalized. Then, switch roles with your partner.

Name _____ Date _____

89 USING CAPITALS IN LETTERS

In letter salutations, capitalize the first word, all names and titles, and all other significant words. In letter closings, capitalize only the first word.

Salutations	Dear Mike,	Dear Ms. Hadley,
	Dear Madam:	Dear Grandfather,
Closings	Best wishes,	
	With affection,	
	Sincerely,	

PRACTICE A Identifying Salutations and Closings

Read each of the following examples of salutations and closings. On the line provided, write S if the example is a salutation or C if the example is a closing.

Example: Dear Sir or Madam:
Answer: S

1. Dear Senator Ryan: _____
2. Sincerely yours, _____
3. Dear Mayor Bradley: _____
4. Dear Mrs. Meadow: _____
5. Your cousin, _____

6. With regards, _____
7. Best wishes, _____
8. Yours truly, _____
9. Dear Mr. Allen: _____
10. Dear Congresswoman Myers: _____

PRACTICE B Capitalizing Salutations and Closings

Read each of the following examples of salutations and closings. On the line provided, rewrite the example, using proper capitalization.

Example: dear grandfather,
Answer: Dear Grandfather,

1. dear drew and charles, _____
2. yours truly, _____
3. dear sir: _____
4. dear uncle alex, _____
5. fondest regards, _____
6. dear samuel, _____
7. best, _____
8. dear ms. finer: _____
9. kind regards, _____
10. dear helene, marilyn, and jody, _____

Writing and Speaking Application

Write four examples of letter salutations and four examples of letter closings. Your examples should be capitalized incorrectly. Read your examples to a partner. Your partner should explain how to capitalize each salutation and closing correctly. Then, switch roles with your partner.

90 USING CAPITALS FOR TITLES

- Capitalize a person's title only when it is used with the person's name or when it is used as a proper name by itself. Relatives are often referred to by titles.

  With a Proper Name: I voted for Mayor Frank.
  As a Proper Name: I appreciated your letter, Grandfather.

- Do <u>not</u> capitalize titles showing family relationships when they are preceded by a possessive noun or pronoun. Likewise, do <u>not</u> capitalize titles when they are used as a general reference. **Examples:** my mother, the mayor of our town

- Capitalize the first word and all other key words (nouns, pronouns, verbs, adjectives, and adverbs) in the titles of books, magazines, newspapers, poems, stories, plays, paintings, and other works of art. **Examples:** *The Crucible,* "Birches"

- Capitalize the names of educational courses when they are language courses or when they are followed by a number or preceded by a proper noun or adjective. Do <u>not</u> capitalize school subjects discussed in a general manner. **Examples:** German, Advanced Algebra, Physics 204, geology.

PRACTICE A Identifying Titles

Read each sentence. Then, underline the capitalized title or titles.

Example: I arranged an interview with Senator Carlson.
Answer: I arranged an interview with <u>Senator</u> Carlson.

1. I look forward to our lunch, Grandmother.
2. Mayor-elect Jones is speaking.
3. She subscribes to *Computer Monthly*.
4. I am seeing Pam Manno, D.D.S.
5. Jon enjoyed Greek and Biology 101.

6. My favorite novel is *The Alchemist.*
7. The orchestra is playing "Ode to Joy."
8. "The Stranger" will be published soon.
9. Secretary of State Patel has arrived.
10. Governor Simon will see them later.

PRACTICE B Capitalizing Titles

Read each sentence. On the line provided, rewrite the sentence, capitalizing titles correctly.

Example: Both mayor Ramirez and governor Amir will attend.
Answer: Both Mayor Ramirez and Governor Amir will attend.

1. Next year, I hope to take honors history, chemistry 105, german, and a physics class.

_____

2. In the audience were mrs. Cardoza, senator Highland, mayor Frank, and an ambassador.

_____

3. The art reviewer praised the paintings *early morning, sunrise on the prairie,* and *high noon.*

_____

4. Although aunt Sylvia is a well-known reporter, she hasn't written for the *harrisville times.*

_____

5. Last night, dr. Myers and congresswoman Benson met with attorney general Harris.

_____

Writing and Speaking Application

Write a short paragraph about your favorite class in school. Use at least four titles that should be capitalized. Then, read your paragraph to a partner. Your partner should identify the titles that should be capitalized. Then, switch roles with your partner.

91 USING PERIODS AS END MARKS

Use a period to end a declarative sentence, a mild imperative sentence, or an indirect question.

See the examples below.

A **declarative** sentence is a statement of fact or opinion.	The dinner was excellent.
An **imperative** sentence gives a direction or a command.	Clear the table.
An **indirect question** restates a question in a declarative sentence.	My mother asked whether I was still hungry.

PRACTICE A Using Periods to End Sentences

Read each sentence. Then, add a period where it is needed.

Example: Sal is a good carpenter
Answer: Sal is a good carpenter.

1. The teacher asked how we did on the test
2. I have not seen the cat today
3. Find it
4. Once you have added the flour, mix the ingredients thoroughly
5. Remember to bring your books home

6. My father asked whether I had sorted the recycling
7. Our team is undefeated
8. Turn off the lights
9. I did not know the answer to the problem
10. Make a right turn onto Main Street

PRACTICE B Using Periods and Identifying Their Functions

Read each sentence. Add a period where it is needed. Then, on the line provided, write whether the item is a declarative sentence, *an* imperative sentence, *or an* indirect question.

Example: Help me paint the fence
Answer: Help me paint the fence. imperative sentence

1. I am a pretty good painter _____

2. Start painting that side _____

3. I would rather paint this side first _____

4. Listen to my instructions _____

5. I am going to college after I graduate _____

6. You should apply in the fall _____

7. I asked whether my grades were high enough to get in _____

8. Study hard _____

9. She asked which test preparation course I had taken _____

10. Preparing thoroughly is a smart idea _____

Writing and Speaking Application

Write two declarative sentences, imperative sentences, and indirect questions. Switch papers with a partner. Take turns reading the sentences aloud and identifying each as a declarative sentence, an imperative sentence, or an indirect question.

92 OTHER USES OF PERIODS

A period can signal that words have been shortened or abbreviated.

Use a period after most abbreviations and after people's initials. Also use periods after numbers and letters in outlines. Do <u>not</u> use periods with initialisms or acronyms, which are formed from the first letter or first few letters of a series of words. See the examples below.

Use periods in abbreviations of titles, place names, times, dates, and people's initials.	Ms., Gov. (Governor), Mon. (Monday), Jan. (January), K. Sanchez, 10:00 P.M., Ave.
Use periods in certain other common abbreviations (in informal writing only).	doz. (dozen), meas. (measure), pg. (page), pp. (pages)
Use periods in outlines.	I. Use Periods A. In Outlines
Do <u>not</u> use periods with most initialisms (which are pronounced letter by letter) or acronyms (which are pronounced as words).	initialisms: USA, UN acronyms: NASA, FEMA
Do <u>not</u> use periods with postal abbreviations of states, metric measurements, or most standard measurements.	FL (Florida), mm (millimeters), qt (quarts) (exception: *in.* for *inches*)

PRACTICE A Using Periods Correctly in Abbreviations

Read each sentence. Then, add any periods that are needed. If none need to be added, write none.

Example: Mr Cosgriff is the father of my best friend, Eric.
Answer: Mr. Cosgriff is the father of my best friend, Eric.

1. Mrs. Holmgren told us that the quiz would be given at 12:30 P.M. sharp. _____

2. My dentist's name is Dr Vasquez. _____

3. The quotation I've been looking for is on pg 348. _____

4. Mrs Garcia called to tell you that work would start at 5:00 PM tomorrow. _____

5. Is Ms Roberts a citizen of the USA or of another country? _____

PRACTICE B Writing Abbreviations Correctly

Read each sentence. On the line provided, correctly write each term that needs a period added or deleted.

Example: My mother leaves for work at 7:10 AM each morning.
Answer: A.M.

1. Is Gov Calderon attending the fundraiser? _____

2. The grocery list included 2 doz eggs. _____

3. After making a left onto Washington Ave, you'll see the new café. _____

4. Her return address is 170 Biondi St, New York, N.Y. 10003. _____

5. The information you need can be found on pp 75–78. _____

Writing and Speaking Application

Write a paragraph that includes at least five abbreviations. Switch papers with a partner. Take turns reading the paragraphs aloud and identifying each abbreviation and its correct punctuation.

93 USING QUESTION MARKS

A question mark should be used after a **direct question**: *Why do you have to leave so early?*

A question mark should be used for an **incomplete question**: *Really? How? Seriously? Why not?*

A question mark should be used for a **statement intended as a question**: *Your title is manager?*

Do <u>not</u> use a question mark with an **indirect question**, which is a <u>statement</u> that contains a question. An incorrectly punctuated indirect question can be fixed by (1) removing the question mark and adding a period or (2) rephrasing the statement so that it is a direct question.

> **Incorrect:** *She asked whether I wanted to go?*
> **Corrected:** *She asked whether I wanted to go.*
> **Incorrect:** *I wonder whether I should go to the play?*
> **Corrected:** *I wonder whether I should go to the play.* **or** *Should I go to the play?*

PRACTICE A Determining Whether to Use Question Marks

Read each sentence. Then, add the correct end mark. Some items may require an end mark other than a question mark.

Example: How could you forget to do your research paper
Answer: How could you forget to do your research paper<u>?</u>

1. How will you explain that to your teacher
2. My father asked me how I could forget
3. Do you think the teacher will understand
4. Why not
5. Can you remember your first day of kindergarten
6. I wonder how long it has been since then
7. How did you lock the keys in the car while it was still running
8. How many colleges will you visit this year
9. Zach asked whether I want to go to college
10. His mother is asking the same question

PRACTICE B Writing Direct Questions Correctly

Read each statement that ends with a question mark. Then, rewrite it as a direct question.

Example: You didn't answer the questions on the back of the test booklet?
Answer: <u>Didn't you answer the questions on the back of the test booklet?</u>

1. There were crumbs on the counter? _____

2. You left the umbrella in the car? _____

3. The dog got out of the house again? _____

4. Hernando pitched a perfect game? _____

5. You knew about your own surprise party? _____

6. You were only pretending to be surprised? _____

7. My sister told my mother that I knew about it? _____

8. The eggs she used in the recipe were fresh? _____

Writing and Speaking Application

Write five statements. Switch papers with a partner. Rewrite your partner's statements as questions. Read the new questions to your partner.

94 USING EXCLAMATION POINTS

Use an exclamation point to end an exclamatory sentence, a forceful imperative sentence, an interjection with emphasis, or any other exclamation. Exclamation points indicate strong emotion and should be used sparingly, especially in formal writing.

See the examples in the chart.

Exclamatory Sentence/Other Exclamation	What a nerve-wracking game that was! I can't believe I won!
Forceful Imperative Sentence	Go up to your room!
Interjection With Emphasis	Wow! That was a great movie.

PRACTICE A Using Exclamation Points Correctly

Read these items. Add exclamation points to show that they express strong emotion. (Some items include two elements that require an exclamation point.)

Example: Hey Be careful with that
Answer: Hey! Be careful with that!

Example: What a lovely day it is
Answer: What a lovely day it is!

1. I can't find my book anywhere
2. Look It's right there
3. Whoops I am so forgetful lately
4. Stop That's so annoying
5. How funny that joke was

6. Remember to call me
7. Go to your room
8. Turn down the music
9. Am I late for class
10. Hurry You're going to be late

PRACTICE B Writing Exclamatory Sentences and Imperative Sentences

Read each sentence. Then, rewrite it as either an exclamatory sentence or a forceful imperative sentence. You may change the words as necessary. Remember to use an exclamation point.

Example: You should listen to me.
Answer: Listen to me!

1. Please put your clothes away. _____

2. Could you please shut the door? _____

3. Keep an eye out for ice on the sidewalk. _____

4. That is a fascinating story. _____

5. It is good to see you. _____

6. Will you let me know when you get there? _____

7. I wish someone would clean up this mess. _____

8. Would you finish your homework? _____

Writing and Speaking Application

Write a paragraph that contains at least five declarative and interrogative sentences. Switch papers with a partner. Rewrite each sentence in the paragraph as either an exclamatory sentence or a strong imperative sentence with an exclamation point. Read the new paragraph to your partner.

95 USING COMMAS WITH COMPOUND SENTENCES

Use a comma before a coordinating conjunction to separate two or more independent, or main, clauses in a sentence.

A compound sentence consists of two or more independent clauses. When the independent clauses are joined by a coordinating conjunction (*and, but, for, nor, or, so,* or *yet*), use a comma to separate them.

Example: My sister Briana is going on a camping trip, but I will not be able to join her.

PRACTICE A Using Commas Correctly in Compound Sentences

Read each sentence. Then, add a comma where it is needed.

Example: The dog chased the squirrel around the yard but the squirrel ran up a tree to safety.
Answer: The dog chased the squirrel around the yard, but the squirrel ran up a tree to safety.

1. I went to a basketball game yesterday with Veronica and I am going to a hockey game today with Peter.

2. I saved enough money to buy my favorite phone but the store no longer carried that model.

3. Mayumi works as a carpenter during the day and she volunteers three nights per week.

4. I can go to the museum with Ahmed or I can go to the skatepark with my cousin.

5. We can take the freeway to the amusement park or we can try the back roads instead.

6. Sunday is my favorite day for it is a time for me to relax.

7. We can do a research paper on the city of our choice or we can do an oral presentation about a famous historic figure.

8. I took my dog for a walk around the lake after school so it was very tired in the evening.

PRACTICE B Using Commas Correctly to Write Compound Sentences

Read each pair of sentences below. Then, combine the sentences into one compound sentence by using a coordinating conjunction and a comma.

Example: The mall was very crowded. We did most of our shopping on the Internet.
Answer: The mall was very crowded, so we did most of our shopping on the Internet.

1. Fernando plays the piano very well. He is also a good violinist.

_____

2. My dog's name is Chelsea. My cat's name is Bromley.

_____

3. My favorite subject is biology. I received a higher grade in geometry.

_____

4. We did not have enough time to finish the science lab. We will have to come back after school.

_____

5. My favorite hobby is chess. I also play video games.

_____

Writing and Speaking Application

Write five sentence pairs. Switch papers with a partner. Use coordinating conjunctions and commas to create a compound sentence from each sentence pair. Take turns reading aloud the new sentences and checking each other's work for correct use of commas.

96 AVOIDING COMMA SPLICES

When two independent clauses are incorrectly joined with only a comma (and no coordinating conjunction), the result is called a **comma splice**. Comma splices are a type of run-on sentence.

> **Comma Splice:** The storm brought over four inches of rain, many streets were flooded.

There are several ways to correct a comma splice: (1) add a coordinating conjunction (*and, but, for, nor, or, so,* or *yet*) after the comma, (2) replace the comma with a semicolon, (3) create multiple sentences, or (4) revise the wording of the sentence.

> **Correct:** The storm brought over four inches of rain. Many streets were flooded.
> **Correct:** The storm brought over four inches of rain, so many streets were flooded.
> **Correct:** The storm brought over four inches of rain; many streets were flooded.

PRACTICE A Correcting Comma Splices

Read each item. Then, rewrite it to eliminate the comma splice. You may need to write two new sentences.

Example: The children are eating their dinner now, I will wait until later to eat mine.
Answer: The children are eating their dinner now, **but** I will wait until later to eat mine.

1. I went to a concert last night with Shana, I am going to a baseball game today.

_____

2. I have two job opportunities, I still haven't decided which one to accept.

_____

3. I can work part-time at the store, I can volunteer at the animal shelter.

_____

4. We have three dogs, I walk them every day.

_____

5. This weekend, I have to finish my research paper, I also have to complete my math homework.

_____

PRACTICE B Using Commas Correctly in Sentences

Read each item. If the item contains a comma splice, rewrite it, inserting a coordinating conjunction. If the item is correct, write correct.

Example: We took our fishing rods to the lake, we decided to swim instead.
Answer: We took our fishing rods to the lake, **but** we decided to swim instead.

1. My throat was sore, I stayed home from school today.

_____

2. We bought only enough groceries to make dinner, so we will have to go back to the supermarket.

_____

3. I am the captain of the basketball team, I play on the soccer team as well.

_____

Writing and Speaking Application

Write a paragraph about your hobbies. Exchange papers with a partner and check each other's work for correct use of commas. Offer advice for correcting comma splices and any other errors.

97 USING COMMAS IN A SERIES

Use commas to separate three or more words, phrases, or clauses in a series.

A series consists of three or more words, phrases, or clauses. Consider these examples:

Series of Words: The items on the grocery list include cereal, milk, orange juice, and lettuce.

Series of Phrases: The recipe said to separate the eggs, to add the milk, and to sift the flour.

Series of Clauses: In my job interview, I stated that I had prior experience, that I had completed a first-aid course, and that I could provide references.

PRACTICE A Using Commas Correctly in a Series of Words or Phrases

Read each sentence. Then, add commas to the series of words or phrases as needed.

Example: At the farmers' market, we saw handmade crafts potted plants and fresh produce.
Answer: At the farmers' market, we saw handmade crafts, potted plants, and fresh produce.

1. My favorite fruits have always been raspberries watermelon kiwi and mango.

2. My favorite activities are modern dance digital photography and adventure travel.

3. At the sporting-goods store, I bought sneakers hiking boots and a new tent.

4. We had time to go to the car wash to take the clothes to the cleaners and to pick up groceries.

5. My best subjects in school are geometry chemistry and music.

6. At the county park, we walked along the stream over the bridge and into the woods.

PRACTICE B Using Commas Correctly in a Series of Subordinate Clauses

Read each sentence. Then, add commas to the series of subordinate clauses as needed.

Example: The teacher explained that we would be graded on content that we had to provide sources for quotations and that we had to include a slideshow.
Answer: The teacher explained that we would be graded on content, that we had to provide sources for quotations, and that we had to include a slideshow.

1. I decided that I would clean my room that I would go to the movies with Frank and that I would spend some time with my grandparents.

2. My sister asked me if she might borrow my blue sweater if she might take my car to her friend's house and if I would lend her $20.

3. The things I love about summer are that I volunteer at an animal shelter that I go to the beach with my friends and that I can sleep late every morning.

4. The things I love about winter are that my brother comes home from college for a month that we spend the holidays together and that we can make a fire in the fireplace.

5. What I enjoy about babysitting is that I spend time with younger children that I make some money and that I show that I am responsible.

Writing and Speaking Application

Write a sentence in which you use at least one series of subordinate clauses. Trade papers with a partner. Read each other's work aloud, checking for correct comma usage.

98 USING COMMAS BETWEEN ADJECTIVES

When you place two or more adjectives before a noun they describe, make sure to use commas correctly.

- Use commas to separate **coordinate adjectives**, which are adjectives of equal rank. Test whether adjectives are equal by switching their order or by placing the word *and* between them. If the meaning of the sentence stays the same, the adjectives are equal.

  Incorrect: The group had a **carefree relaxed** discussion.
  Correct: The group had a **carefree, relaxed** discussion.

- Don't use commas to separate **cumulative adjectives,** which must have a specific order. By type, cumulative adjectives should appear in the following order: (1) quantity, (2) opinion, (3), size/measurements, (4) age, (5) shape, (6) color, (7) proper adjectives (ethnicity, religion, etc.), (8) material, and (9) purpose.

  Incorrect Order: There are **black large three** crows in the tree.
  Correct Order: There are **three large black** crows in the tree.

- Don't use a comma between the last adjective in a series and the noun it modifies.

  Incorrect: Ahmed started the **rusty, creaking,** tractor.
  Correct: Ahmed started the **rusty, creaking** tractor.

PRACTICE A Using Commas Correctly Between Adjectives

Read each sentence. Then, add commas between adjectives as needed. If the sentence is correct, write correct.

Example: Many famous athletes attended the Super Bowl.
Answer: <u>correct</u>

1. The short asphalt driveway led to the cottage. _____

2. The funny smart speaker held our attention. _____

3. For my birthday, Jamal gave me a beautiful gray jacket. _____

4. Maria bought four wooden chairs for her apartment. _____

5. We used sweet delicious apples to make the pie. _____

PRACTICE B Using Commas Correctly With Adjectives

Read each sentence. Then, add or delete commas as needed. If the sentence is correct, write correct.

Example: We listened to the cheerful happy birds.
Answer: We listened to the cheerful, happy birds.

1. Zach plays his large, red, drums very loudly. _____

2. I thanked Enrique for the thoughtful generous gift. _____

3. There are ten, old, stone cottages in the village. _____

4. I bought five large tomatoes at the farmers' market. _____

5. The museum recently added a beautiful French painting to its collection. _____

Writing and Speaking Application

Write six sentences—each with multiple adjectives. Read your sentences to a partner and check each other's work for correct use of commas between adjectives.

99 USING COMMAS AFTER INTRODUCTORY MATERIAL

Use a comma after an introductory word, phrase, or clause.

Introductory material is any word, phrase, or clause that comes before the main clause of a sentence. See the examples below.

Introductory Words	Yes, you can come with me.
Nouns of Address	Lina, hand me the car keys.
Introductory Adverbs	Eventually, she arrived at school.
Introductory Phrases	To write a good report, I will have to do research.
Adverbial Clauses	If you like sports cars, you will like Tyler's new car.

PRACTICE A Using Commas Correctly With Introductory Material

Read each sentence. Then, add a comma after introductory material as needed.

Example: Yes I am concerned about getting a job this summer.
Answer: Yes, I am concerned about getting a job this summer.

1. Because I was sick I was absent from school.
2. In the library the entire class was quiet.
3. Oh I forgot to ask you to renew that book.
4. Well I did renew it for you.
5. In the new book I am reading I found three stories that I had already read.
6. So why are you bothering reading it at all?
7. Considering how much I like to read I figured I would finish it quickly.
8. True you are an avid and fast reader.
9. Hey did you notice my new hairstyle?
10. Yes it looks really great.

PRACTICE B Using Commas Correctly in Sentences With Introductory Material

Read each sentence. Then, add a comma after introductory material as needed.

Example: Sure I think going to the lake on Saturday is a great idea.
Answer: Sure, I think going to the lake on Saturday is a great idea.

1. Well I will have to ask my father if I can borrow his car.

2. While you are at it why don't you ask him if you can borrow his fishing gear?

3. Carly do you really think he would lend me his fishing gear?

4. Hey you'll never know unless you ask.

5. Considering how much my father loves to fish I doubt he will say yes.

6. Because of the heat wave classes are canceled for the afternoon.

7. While I was staying with my grandmother I found some great photographs in the attic.

8. Wow what else did you find?

9. Although most of her things were covered with old sheets I did find an antique lamp.

10. Oh do you think your grandmother will give it to you?

Writing and Speaking Application

With a partner, write a four-line dialogue between two people on the topic of your choice. Each line of dialogue should contain introductory material. Work together to edit your dialogue for correct use of commas with introductory material. Then, read your dialogue to the class.

100 USING COMMAS WITH PARENTHETICAL EXPRESSIONS

Use a comma or commas to set off a parenthetical expression from the rest of the sentence.

A parenthetical expression is a word or phrase that interrupts the flow of a sentence. Use two commas to set off a parenthetical expression in the middle of a sentence. Only one comma is needed to set off a parenthetical expression at the end of a sentence. See the examples below.

Noun of Direct Address	Can you recommend a good restaurant, <u>Mrs. Wells</u>?
Conjunctive Adverb	I can, <u>indeed</u>, recommend an excellent restaurant.
Common Expression	You all like Mexican food, <u>I assume</u>.
Contrasting Expression	We have to go to a place that is in walking, <u>not driving</u>, distance.

PRACTICE A Using Correct Comma Placement With Contrasting Expressions

Read each sentence. Then, add a comma or commas to set off the contrasting expression.

Example: Shane is looking for a part-time not a full-time job.
Answer: Shane is looking for a part-time, not a full-time, job.

1. He should look in the county newspaper not the town newspaper.

2. Adam wants to work in construction not in landscaping.

3. He will have to be flexible not rigid in his job search.

4. Malika is best friends with Vicki not with Carla.

5. My sister goes to a state college not a private one.

6. Zach's twin brother's name is Justin not Dustin.

7. The tree in our backyard is a pear tree not a crabapple tree.

8. The flowers on the tree are white not pink.

PRACTICE B Using Commas Correctly With Parenthetical Expressions

Read each sentence. Then, rewrite it, adding or deleting a comma as needed. If the sentence is correct, write correct.

Example: My brother is concentrating his studies on math not science.
Answer: My brother is concentrating his studies on math, not science.

1. I am taking Spanish not Latin this year. _____

2. That I believe is a, good, idea. _____

3. It is a good idea, indeed, considering I want to travel to Spain.

_____

4. You should therefore study hard to master the language.

_____

5. Latin however may help you, expand, your vocabulary.

_____

Writing and Speaking Application

Write six sentences using commas to set off parenthetical expressions. With a partner, read the sentences aloud and take turns identifying the parenthetical expressions.

101 USING COMMAS WITH NONRESTRICTIVE EXPRESSIONS

Use a comma or commas to set off a nonrestrictive, or nonessential, expression.

A nonrestrictive expression can be left out of a sentence without changing the meaning of the sentence. Use two commas to set off a nonrestrictive expression in the middle of a sentence. Only one comma is needed to set off a nonrestrictive expression at the end of a sentence. See the examples below.

Nonrestrictive Appositive Phrase	The book was written by Ernest Hemingway, the famous author.
Nonrestrictive Participial Phrase	The story, written in 1951, is about an old man and the sea.
Nonrestrictive Adjectival Clause	The title, which describes the plot, is *The Old Man and the Sea*.

PRACTICE A Using Correct Comma Placement With Nonrestrictive Expressions

Read each sentence. Then, add a comma or commas to set off the nonrestrictive expression.

Example: The shopping center which is five blocks away has a grocer, a barber, and a tailor.
Answer: The shopping center, which is five blocks away, has a grocer, a barber, and a tailor.

1. A new movie theater the only one for miles opened just a few months ago.

2. I've seen about have a dozen movies there with my best friend Suzanne.

3. Suzanne's mother who works in a doctor's office usually picks us up afterward.

4. My baseball coach who has three young children knows the stats of all the major-league players.

5. Simone Girard a senior was voted school treasurer.

6. Simone who is originally from Haiti is an excellent math student.

7. The concert which is tomorrow night should be fun and well attended.

8. Our new car which is black with a tan interior is parked in the garage.

9. The meal which was served at 7:00 P.M. consisted of chicken, broccoli, and mushrooms.

10. The house next door built in the 1950s has recently been renovated.

PRACTICE B Using Commas Correctly With Nonrestrictive Expressions

Read each sentence. Then, add commas as needed. If the sentence is correct, write correct.

Example: My grandparents who have been married for fifty years are wonderful people.
Answer: My grandparents, who have been married for fifty years, are wonderful people.

1. My locker which is 18 inches wide is on the second floor of the school. _____

2. My cousin's school only three miles from here accepts 100 new students a year. _____

3. My favorite poem, a true classic, is "The Road Not Taken." _____

4. The frozen lake which is perfect for skating is about 10 miles from here. _____

5. The lasagna which is a family recipe is baking in the oven. _____

Writing and Speaking Application

Write a paragraph about what you did last weekend. Use commas incorrectly with nonrestrictive expressions. Exchange papers with a partner and correct the comma placement. Read aloud the corrected paragraphs.

102 USING COMMAS WITH DATES, GEOGRAPHICAL NAMES, AND TITLES

Use a comma or commas with a multipart date, a multipart geographical name, or a title that follows a person's name.

- If a date includes a month, a day, and a year, use a comma or commas to set off the year. If a date does not include all three parts, no commas are needed.
- If a geographical name includes two parts, such as both a city and a state or country, use a comma or commas to set off the second part.
- If one or more titles (such as *Jr., Sr., Esq., M.D.,* or *Ph.D.*) follow a person's name, use a comma or commas to set off each title.

See the examples below.

Date With Commas	The building will be closed from December 23, 2022, through January 2, 2023.
Date Without Commas	I visited Arizona in June 2019 and in May 2021. I'm flying there again on April 16 this year.
Geographical Name	My mother flew from Atlanta, Georgia, to Berlin, Germany, for business.
Name With One or More Titles	J. Gutierrez, Jr., Ph.D., was one of my college professors.

PRACTICE A Using Commas Correctly With Dates, Geographical Names, and Titles

Read the sentences. Then, add a comma or commas as needed to correctly punctuate any date, geographical name, or title. If a sentence is correct, write correct.

Example: The art gallery is called Nova, and it is located in San Antonio Texas.
Answer: The art gallery is called Nova, and it is located in San Antonio, Texas.

1. The building in Philadelphia, Pennsylvania, is dated July 16, 1988. _____

2. Christopher Jones Jr. is our music teacher. _____

3. Judith Frankel Ph.D. is my sister's psychology professor. _____

4. Many tourists visit the Eifel Tower when they are in Paris France. _____

5. The town swim club first opened on May 10 2017. _____

PRACTICE B Writing Sentences With Dates, Geographical Names, and Titles

Read each item. Then, write a sentence with it. Be sure to use commas correctly.

Example: Rome Italy
Answer: If I get the chance to travel to Rome, Italy, I'd love to see the Colosseum.

1. Nelson Taylor Jr. _____

2. Colette Brador Ph.D. _____

3. Denver Colorado _____

4. October 31 2021 _____

Writing and Speaking Application

Write five sentences using dates, geographical locations, and titles. Do not include commas.
Exchange papers with a partner and add commas to each other's sentences as needed. Then, discuss the corrections.

103 USING COMMAS IN NUMBERS

Use a comma or commas to separate groups of three digits in large numbers.

Commas make large numbers easier to read by grouping the digits. In general, with large numbers of more than three digits, use a comma after every third digit starting from the right. However, do <u>not</u> use commas in ZIP codes, telephone numbers, page numbers, years, serial numbers, or house numbers. See the examples below.

Use commas in large numbers of more than three digits.	7,898 books 10,877 songs 1,909,498 residents	
Do <u>not</u> use commas in ZIP codes, telephone numbers, page numbers, years, serial numbers, or house numbers.	ZIP code 02334 (222) 757-9944 Page 1002	Year 2014 Serial number 444095826 2256 Gramercy Place

PRACTICE A Using Correct Comma Placement in Numbers

Read each item. Then, rewrite the item, correcting any improper comma usage. If the item is correct, write correct.

Example: 1011 students
Answer: <u>1,011 students</u>

1. 1,614 Bayview Road _____
2. year 1850 _____
3. (802) 664-7694 _____
4. 1044 members _____
5. 4359 voters _____

6. (202) 272-8,777 _____
7. October 13, 2,004 _____
8. serial number 333,111,909 _____
9. 1815 Cleveland Road _____
10. March 10, 1,992 _____

PRACTICE B Writing Sentences Using Commas in Numbers

Read each number. Then, include it in a sentence of your own, using it as indicated in parentheses. Be sure to use commas correctly in numbers.

Example: 20885 (large number)
Answer: <u>There were 20,885 fans at the concert.</u>

1. 2499 (house number) _____
2. 146243978 (serial number) _____
3. (212) 531-9786 (telephone number) _____
4. 00433 (ZIP code) _____
5. 5049287 (large number) _____
6. 2012 (page number) _____

Writing and Speaking Application

Write a brief paragraph in which you include large numbers and dates. Do not include commas. Exchange papers with a partner and add commas to each other's paragraphs as needed. Then, take turns reading the correctly punctuated paragraphs aloud.

104 USING COMMAS WITH ADDRESSES AND IN LETTERS

Use commas to punctuate specific parts of addresses and letters.

Commas are used in addresses, salutations of friendly letters, and closings of friendly or business letters. See the examples below for when to use commas in addresses and letters.

On an envelope or at the top of a letter, use a comma between the city and the state's postal abbreviation. (When applicable, also use a comma between the street address and the apartment number.)	Mrs. Kelly McColl 42 Kenlot Place, Apt. 6D Austin, TX 73344
In a sentence, use a comma after each element of the address, other than the state's postal abbreviation.	Send a note to Mrs. Kelly McColl, 42 Kenlot Place, Apt. 6D, Austin, TX 73344.
Use a comma after the salutation in a friendly letter and after the closing in all letters.	Dear Joe, Yours truly, Dear Grandma, Sincerely,

PRACTICE A Using Correct Comma Placement in Letters

Read each salutation or closing. Then, revise comma usage as needed. If the item is correct, write correct.

Example: Dear Kenji

Answer: Dear Kenji,

1. Fondly, _____
2. Sincerely _____
3. Dear Uncle Miguel _____

4. Best wishes _____
5. Sincerely, yours _____
6. With warmest regards _____

PRACTICE B Using Commas in Addresses

Read each address. Write it as it would appear on an envelope, deleting commas as needed.

Example: Len Frankel, 67 Emmett Place, San Diego, CA 42987

Answer: Len Frankel
67 Emmett Place
San Diego, CA 42987

1. Trudy Garcia, 978 Elm Street, Trumbel, CT 98754

_____

_____

_____

3. Zach McCollum, 89 Kent Road, Apt. 9E, Glen Ridge, AL 08654

_____

_____

_____

2. Skye Bernhardt, 922 Laurel Avenue, Apt. 402, River Edge, AZ 75634

_____

_____

_____

4. David Huang, 46 Lake Harbor Road, Lake Harbor, MI 56231

_____

_____

_____

Writing and Speaking Application

Write a brief friendly letter to a person of your choice. Use commas correctly. Exchange papers with a partner and check for correct use of commas. Then, take turns reading your correctly punctuated letters aloud.

105 USING COMMAS IN ELLIPTICAL SENTENCES

Use a comma in place of the word or words omitted from an elliptical sentence.

In an **elliptical sentence**, the structures of two adjacent independent clauses are so similar that a word or words may be omitted from the second clause, rather than repeated, and the sentence will still be understood. Use a comma in place of the omitted word or words. See the example below.

Use a comma to indicate the word or words left out of an elliptical sentence.	Marcus made three drawings; Ella, two paintings. *(Marcus made three drawings; Ella made two paintings.)*

PRACTICE A Using Correct Comma Placement in Elliptical Sentences

Read each elliptical sentence. Then, add a comma where it is needed.

Example: The juniors park in the south parking lot; the seniors the north parking lot.
Answer: The juniors park in the south parking lot; the seniors, the north parking lot.

1. Lunch is sixth period; study hall ninth period.

2. My apartment building is on Crawford Avenue; my grandmother's on Main Street.

3. Our family has a gray car; my aunt a white one.

4. The middle school is on Maple Avenue; the high school on Grand Street.

5. The hardware store is on the west side of the street; the bank the east side of the street.

6. The hockey rink seats about 500 people; the football stadium about 1,000 people.

7. My bedroom is on the second floor; my brother's the first floor.

8. My favorite type of food is Mexican; my sister's Italian.

9. This year, I am taking Spanish; next year French.

10. In the summer, I work at the town pool; in the winter at the coffee shop.

PRACTICE B Using Commas Correctly in Elliptical Sentences

Rewrite each sentence to form an elliptical sentence, adding a semicolon and an elliptical clause with a comma.

Example: The junior prom was held on Friday night.
Answer: The junior prom was held on Friday night; the senior prom, on Saturday night.

1. Luis went to the basketball courts.

_____

2. My cousins live in Alabama.

_____

3. My brother plays jazz guitar.

_____

4. I received three phone calls last night.

_____

5. I leave for school at 8:15 every morning.

_____

Writing and Speaking Application

Write five elliptical sentences. Leave out the commas. Switch papers with a partner and correct each other's sentences. Then, take turns reading your correctly punctuated sentences aloud.

106 USING COMMAS WITH DIRECT QUOTATIONS

Commas are used to show where direct quotations begin and end.

Use commas to set off a direct quotation from the rest of the sentence. See the examples below.

"Don't forget to pick your sister up after school," my mother said, "because she is not taking the bus today."

I replied, "OK, Mom. No problem."

"Great," answered Mom. "Drive safely and have a good day at school."

PRACTICE A Using Correct Comma Placement With Direct Quotations

Read each direct quotation. Then, rewrite it, adding a comma or commas as needed.

Example: "I can help you fix the car" I told my father.
Answer: "I can help you fix the car," I told my father.

1. "Great" he replied. "Grab a wrench from the toolbox." _____
_____

2. I answered "This will be good practice for my auto mechanics class." _____
_____

3. He said "It works out well for me, too." _____
_____

4. "I am going to the movies with Jackie and Tim tonight" I told my sister. _____
_____

5. "Well, I hope you don't plan on taking the car" she answered "because I need it." ___
_____

PRACTICE B Using Commas Correctly With Direct Quotations

Read each item. Then, rewrite it as a direct quotation, adding quotation marks and a comma or commas as needed. For your new sentence, add a speaker of the quotation, as in the example shown.

Example: This painting was made during the Renaissance.
Answer: "This painting was made during the Renaissance," explained the tour guide.

1. I have just enough money to buy a new gaming console. _____

2. Last night, we heard an owl hooting. _____

3. This bus is never on time. _____

4. Let's meet at the basketball court after school. _____

5. This new app helps me track my workouts. _____

Writing and Speaking Application

Work with a partner to write a brief dialogue. Use direct quotations, and be sure to correctly place the commas. Then, read your dialogue aloud together.

107 USING COMMAS FOR CLARITY

Using commas correctly helps improve clarity.

The rules for comma usage are not arbitrary. Rather, they are meant to aid readers.

Recall that a comma should be used after introductory material—any word, phrase, or subordinate clause that comes before the main clause in a sentence. One of the reasons to use a comma in this way is to make the sentence clear for readers.

Consider the example below. Without the comma, a reader might read "fire alarms" as a compound noun. The reader would then have to reread the sentence to figure out the intended meaning. Placing a comma after the introductory clause aids the reader by improving clarity.

> **Unclear:** After we put out the fire alarms stopped ringing.

> **Clear:** After we put out the fire, alarms stopped ringing.

PRACTICE A Inserting Commas for Clarity

Read each sentence. Then, add a comma where it is needed for clarity.

Example: For the group meetings were scheduled.
Answer: For the group, meetings were scheduled.

1. During the flight attendants served us lunch.
2. Standing near the airplane pilots discussed the flight path.
3. Before the holiday shoppers looked for bargains.
4. For the parade on Halloween costumes were worn by all.
5. At the ocean waves crashed against the wall.

6. To improve in tennis players must practice often.
7. To be prepared for going to the gym bags must be packed the night before.
8. Though roses are red violets are blue.
9. As the students were crossing guards stopped traffic.
10. As we watched the rain drops streamed down the window.

PRACTICE B Writing Sentences With Commas Used for Clarity

Read each word pair. Then, write a sentence in which a comma separates the words, improving clarity.

Example: college applications
Answer: For that college, applications must be received by November.

1. counter stools _____
2. party decorations _____
3. floating balloons _____
4. broken umbrellas _____
5. park rangers _____
6. sleeping bags _____
7. assembled objects _____
8. lamp shades _____

Writing and Speaking Application

Write five sentences that require commas for clarity, but leave the commas out. Then, switch papers with a partner. Add commas to your partner's sentences. Take turns reading aloud your correctly punctuated sentences.

Name _____ Date _____

108 MISUSES OF COMMAS

Avoid using unnecessary commas.

Commas are used so frequently that sometimes writers insert commas that are unnecessary. Note the deletion of misused commas in the examples below.

Misused With an Adjective and a Noun	**Original:** I carried my heavy, bulky, bag. **Revised:** I carried my heavy, bulky bag.
Misused With a Compound Subject	**Original:** My cousin, and I, went to our grandparents' house. **Revised:** My cousin and I went to our grandparents' house.
Misused With a Compound Verb	**Original:** He cooked dinner, and read his little brother a story. **Revised:** He cooked dinner and read his little brother a story.
Misused With a Compound Object	**Original:** She wore gloves, and a hat, while shoveling snow. **Revised:** She wore gloves and a hat while shoveling snow.
Misused With Phrases and Clauses	**Original:** Having finished her homework, and having cleaned her room, Sheila decided it was time to relax. **Revised:** Having finished her homework and having cleaned her room, Sheila decided it was time to relax.

PRACTICE A Correcting Misused Commas in Sentences

Read each sentence. Then, delete the misused comma or commas as shown in the example.

Example: We invited Craig, Stephanie, and Elena, over for dinner.
Answer: We invited Craig, Stephanie, and Elena over for dinner.

1. We added peppers, onions, and mushrooms, to the omelet.
2. My aunt, and my mother, planned the vacation to Mexico together.
3. Thinking about the soft sand, and the warm ocean water, made me excited for the trip.
4. I will go either to the shoe store downtown, or to the one in the mall.
5. I request grapes, instead of apples.
6. Neither Mrs. Sheppard, nor the children, were in the store.

PRACTICE B Writing Sentences Without Misusing Commas

Read each set of words or phrases. Then, use the set in a sentence as indicated in parentheses. Be sure not to misuse commas.

Example: suitcase, backpack (compound subject)
Answer: The suitcase and the backpack are still in the taxi.

1. apples, oranges, lemons (compound object) _____
2. talked, laughed (compound verb) _____
3. reading the book, writing the report (phrases or clauses) _____
4. breakfast, lunch, dinner (compound subject) _____
5. working, studying, relaxing (compound verb) _____

Writing and Speaking Application

Write four sentences with unnecessary commas. Switch papers with a partner and delete any unnecessary commas. Take turns reading aloud the correctly punctuated sentences and discuss the corrections that you each made.

109 USING SEMICOLONS TO JOIN INDEPENDENT CLAUSES

Use a semicolon (;) to join two or more closely related independent clauses.

If the ideas in two or more independent clauses are closely related, they can be joined by a semicolon, rather than by a comma and a coordinating conjunction. However, do not use a semicolon to connect two unrelated independent clauses. Use a period or another end mark instead. See the examples below.

Use a semicolon to connect related independent clauses that are not already joined by the coordinating conjunction *and, but, for, nor, or, so,* or *yet.*	Gretchen has a dog; Carla has a cat. Gretchen has a dog; Carla has a cat; Juan has both.
Use a semicolon to join independent clauses separated by either a conjunctive adverb (such as *also, besides, first, however, instead, then, therefore*) or a transitional expression (such as *in fact, as a result, on the other hand*).	Our car won't be fixed until tomorrow; therefore, we have to take the bus today.

PRACTICE A Using Semicolons to Connect Independent Clauses

Read each pair or group of independent clauses. If the independent clauses are closely related, rewrite them as a single sentence using a semicolon or semicolons. If they are unrelated, write unrelated.

Example: On Monday, we have chicken. On Tuesday, we have pasta. On Wednesday, we have tacos.
Answer: On Monday, we have chicken; on Tuesday, we have pasta; on Wednesday, we have tacos.

1. We finished reading *Hamlet*. We are moving on to *Macbeth*.

_____

2. I have two brothers. They are twins. _____

3. I had a little fender-bender today. I learned to drive a few years ago.

_____

4. Tonight, we are going to a show. Tomorrow, we are going to the game. Sunday, we are staying home.

_____

5. My friends like to go shopping. My uncle Eduardo is traveling to Ohio next week.

_____

PRACTICE B Using Semicolons With Conjunctive Adverbs and Transitional Expressions

Read each pair of independent clauses. Rewrite the pair as a single sentence, using a semicolon to correctly separate the independent clauses.

Example: I have researched cars for months. Therefore, I know which one I am going to buy.
Answer: I have researched cars for months; therefore, I know which one I am going to buy.

1. I was tired. Consequently, I fell right to sleep. _____

2. I like to water-ski. Moreover, I like to swim. _____

3. My brother had to work late. Therefore, I had to wait for him to pick me up.

_____

4. Max thought he had his keys. However, he had locked himself out.

Writing and Speaking Application

Write five pairs of related independent clauses. Switch papers with a partner. Combine each pair into a single sentence, using a semicolon to separate the independent clauses. Read the sentences aloud and discuss the changes.

110 USING SEMICOLONS TO AVOID CONFUSION

Use a semicolon (;) to separate sentence elements that already contain commas.

When independent clauses or items in a series already contain commas of their own, using a semicolon to separate them instead of a comma can help prevent confusion. See the examples below.

Use semicolons to separate independent clauses that contain commas.	Walter Nicholas, a noted explorer, has signed a contract with a major television network; he will narrate a series of one-hour shows to be aired next fall.
Use semicolons to separate items in a series when the items contain commas.	The apartment has a bedroom, which has a large closet; a bathroom, which has a double sink; and a kitchen, which has a new stove.

PRACTICE A Using Semicolons to Avoid Confusion in Sentences

Read each sentence. Then, rewrite it, inserting a semicolon or semicolons where needed.

Example: The new phone comes with a case, which helps to protect it, a charger, which has a three-foot-long cable, and a two-year warranty, which covers mechanical failures.

Answer: The new phone comes with a case, which helps to protect it; a charger, which has a three-foot-long cable; and a two-year warranty, which covers mechanical failures.

1. The apartment, which contained only one bedroom, was too small to house any more pets, moreover, another dog would make her allergies even worse.

_____

2. While on vacation, I sent postcards to Maria, who lives in Iowa, Noah, who lives in Oregon, and Isabel, who lives in Georgia.

_____

3. If you need to take a bus uptown, you can take the 506, which leaves from Main Street, the 811, which leaves from Elm Street, or the 904, which leaves from Maple Avenue.

_____

4. Lisa Chen, an experienced engineer, will be the first speaker, Marco Ramirez, a math professor, will be the second speaker, and Olivia Khan, an accounting expert, will be the third speaker.

_____

PRACTICE B Writing Sentences With Semicolons

Read each word group. Then, write a complete sentence in which you include the word group, using semicolons to avoid confusion.

Example: brown jacket, leather briefcase, black shoes

Answer: The man, who looked wealthy, wore a brown jacket and carried a leather briefcase; however, his black shoes were unpolished.

1. bat, ball, glove _____
2. clarinet, flute, piano _____
3. school, career, family _____
4. to draw, to paint, to photograph _____

Writing and Speaking Application

Write two sentences in which you include items in a series. Do not include semicolons in your sentences. Switch papers with a partner. Use semicolons correctly to edit your partner's sentences. Take turns reading aloud the new sentences.

111 USING COLONS

A colon (:) is used to introduce a list of items and in certain other special situations.

Use a colon after an independent clause to introduce a list of items.	To fix the door, we needed the following items: a level, a saw, a hammer, and two nails.
Use a colon to introduce a formal or lengthy quotation or one that does not have a speaker tag (such as *I said*).	As Plato, the philosopher, once said: "Good people do not need laws to tell them to act responsibly, while bad people will find a way around the laws."
Use a colon to introduce a sentence that summarizes or explains the sentence before it. Capitalize the first word in each.	I had a very good reason for not calling you last night: My mother was on the phone with my grandmother for two hours.
Use a colon to introduce a formal appositive that follows an independent clause.	We finally decided where we would go on vacation: Orlando, Florida.
Use a colon in numerals giving the time, salutations in business letters, and references to periodicals and the Bible.	3:23 P.M. Dear Madam: *Scientific American* 42:12

PRACTICE A Using Colons in Sentences

Read each sentence. Then, insert a colon or colons where needed.

Example: I finally decided which foreign language to take next year Spanish.
Answer: I finally decided which foreign language to take next year: Spanish.

1. Chemistry class begins at 11 40 A.M. and ends at 12 25 P.M.

2. I cited the article I had used in the report as *National Geographic* 74 10.

3. The supermarket is open every day from 6 30 A.M. until 11 30 P.M.

4. I made up my mind about which college to attend University of Texas, Austin.

5. The reason I chose the school was obvious It has the best biology department.

6. At the mall, we went to the following places the theater, the food court, and the shoe store.

7. We are having the following appetizers at the party dim sum, spring rolls, and miso soup.

8. Can you pick your sister up from school at 3 25 P.M.?

PRACTICE B Writing With Colons

Read each item. Then, write an example, using a colon in the way the item indicates.

Example: to introduce an appositive that follows an independent clause
Answer: Simon had decided what to have for lunch: a sandwich.

1. to indicate time _____

2. to introduce a long quotation _____

3. to cite an article in a periodical _____

4. to summarize the sentence before it _____

5. in a salutation of a business letter _____

Writing and Speaking Application

Write a business letter requesting an upgrade for your phone. Use at least five sentences that need colons, but leave out the colons. Switch papers with a partner. Edit your partner's letter, adding colons where needed. Take turns reading aloud the edited letters.

112 USING QUOTATION MARKS WITH QUOTATIONS

Use quotation marks to set off a person's exact words.

Quotation marks are used to set off a **direct quotation**, which represents a person's exact words, thoughts, or writing. On the other hand, an **indirect quotation**, which reports the general meaning of what a person says, thinks, or writes, should not be set off with quotation marks. See the examples below.

A direct quotation is enclosed in quotation marks.	"Why didn't you finish the project?" I asked Geraldo.
An indirect quotation does not require quotation marks.	Geraldo said that he had completely forgotten about it.

PRACTICE A Using Quotation Marks With Direct Quotations

Read each item. Then, insert quotation marks where needed.

Example: A stranger walked up to me and asked, Do you know where the bus stop is?
Answer: A stranger walked up to me and asked, "Do you know where the bus stop is?"

1. My father asked, Has anyone seen my toolbox?
2. My mother answered, No, I never use the toolbox.
3. I saw it in the garage, Dad, I told him.
4. I thought it was there, too, explained my father, but it isn't.
5. My father said, I think I need glasses!
6. What time is the movie playing? Kayla asked.
7. I'm not sure, I answered. Let's check on the Internet.
8. How are we going to get to the theater? Tim asked.

PRACTICE B Identifying Direct Quotations and Indirect Quotations

Read each item. If it is a direct quotation, rewrite it with quotation marks. If it is an indirect quotation, write indirect quotation.

Example: My guidance counselor said that I have to raise my test scores to get into college.
Answer: indirect quotation

1. Maybe you should take a test preparation course, suggested Rachel.

   _____

2. I told Rachel that I agreed with her.

   _____

3. How many weeks are left before the next test? I asked her.

   _____

4. The next test isn't until September of our senior year, she answered.

   _____

5. Well, that's a relief, I replied.

   _____

Writing and Speaking Application

Work with a partner to write an eight-line dialogue about your after-school plans. Use quotation marks around your direct quotations. Then, read aloud your dialogue with your partner.

113 USING SPEAKER TAGS WITH DIRECT QUOTATIONS

A speaker tag may come before, in the middle of, or after a direct quotation.

Generally, a writer identifies the speaker of a direct quotation by using words such as *I said* or *they asked*. These types of expressions are called **speaker tags**, and they may introduce (come before), interrupt (come in the middle of), or conclude (come after) direct quotations. This chart shows some common rules for punctuating speaker tags.

Use a comma after a short speaker tag that introduces a direct quotation.	My sister said, "I will drive you to school today."
Use a colon after a very long or formal speaker tag that introduces a direct quotation.	Civil-rights activist Martin Luther King, Jr., once said: "In the end, we will remember not the words of our enemies but the silence of our friends."
Use two commas when a speaker tag interrupts a speaker's sentence—one after the first part of the direct quotation and one after the speaker tag.	"I will drive you to school today," said my sister, "because I just got my license."
Use a comma, a question mark, or an exclamation point after a direct quotation that is concluded by a speaker tag.	"No thanks. I'd rather walk to school today," I replied.

PRACTICE A Using Punctuation Marks With Speaker Tags

Read each item. Then, rewrite it, inserting quotation marks and a comma or commas where needed.

Example: My mother asked What does everyone want for dinner tonight?
Answer: My mother asked, "What does everyone want for dinner tonight?"

1. I would like chicken I answered. _____

2. Well replied my brother I would rather have meatloaf. _____

3. My sister said I don't like meatloaf, but I like pasta. _____

4. I don't know why I bothered asking my mother said. _____

5. I said I have to finish my research paper. _____

PRACTICE B Writing With Speaker Tags

For each item, write a direct quotation of your own, using quotation marks and other punctuation marks as needed. Place the speaker tag where indicated.

Example: Concluding speaker tag
Answer: "I am happy to tell you that you got the job!" exclaimed the store manager.

1. Introductory speaker tag _____

2. Interrupting speaker tag _____

3. Formal introductory speaker tag _____

4. Concluding speaker tag _____

5. Introductory speaker tag _____

Writing and Speaking Application

Work with a partner to write an eight-line dialogue on the topic of your choice. Use each of the four types of speaker tags at least once: introductory, formal introductory, interrupting, and concluding. Then, read aloud your dialogue with your partner.

114 USING QUOTATION MARKS WITH OTHER PUNCTUATION MARKS

The location of quotation marks in relation to other punctuation marks varies. See the examples below.

Place a comma or a period inside the final quotation mark.	"That is one fabulous necklace," my cousin said. My cousin said, "That is one fabulous necklace."
Place a semicolon or a colon outside the final quotation mark.	I had just bought the "fabulous necklace": I was pleased she liked it.
If a direct quotation is itself a question or an exclamation, place a question mark or an exclamation point <u>inside</u> the final quotation mark. If a direct quotation is a statement, but the surrounding text is a question or an exclamation, place a question mark or an exclamation point <u>outside</u> the final quotation mark.	My cousin asked, "Would you mind if I bought one for myself?" Did he say, "I bought one, too"?

PRACTICE A Using Quotation Marks With Other Punctuation Marks in Sentences

Read each item. Then, insert quotation marks where needed.

Example: The little boy asked, How much is a Popsicle?
Answer: The little boy asked, <u>"How much is a Popsicle?"</u>

1. You have enough money for a Popsicle, I told the boy.

2. Juan shut the book and exclaimed, That is the best book I have ever read!

3. May I borrow the keys to the car? I asked my mother.

4. Have the car back by 8:30, my mother answered.

5. You should bring your math book home tonight to study, Peter reminded me.

6. Good idea! I answered. Thanks for reminding me.

7. Hi, Mom! I shouted. What's for lunch?

8. I made quiche and salad, she said.

9. I have to eat quickly, I told her, because I have to work today.

10. Oh! she exclaimed. I had hoped you would help me with dinner.

PRACTICE B Writing Sentences With Quotation Marks and Other Punctuation Marks

For each item, write a sentence of your own, using quotation marks and the other punctuation mark(s) indicated.

Example: quotation marks, exclamation point
Answer: <u>"I can't believe she said that about me!" exclaimed Cordelia.</u>

1. quotation marks, comma _____

2. quotation marks, semicolon _____

3. quotation marks, commas _____

4. quotation marks, period _____

5. quotation marks, exclamation point _____

Writing and Speaking Application

Work with a partner to write an eight-line dialogue on the topic of your choice. Use the following punctuation marks as well as quotation marks: comma, exclamation point, question mark, period. Then, read aloud your dialogue with your partner.

115 USING SINGLE QUOTATION MARKS FOR QUOTATIONS WITHIN QUOTATIONS

Use single quotation marks (' ') to set off a quotation within a quotation.

Double quotation marks should enclose the main quotation in a sentence. Use single quotation marks to set off a quotation within a quotation. See the example below.

> Michael said, "Ben, did you hear Mrs. Hemmerling say, 'There is no homework tonight'? I thought we had to prepare our oral reports for tomorrow."

PRACTICE A Punctuating Quotations Within Quotations

Read each item. Then, insert single quotation marks where needed.

Example: My sister asked, "Did Dad just say, You can take my car?"
Answer: My sister asked, "Did Dad just say, 'You can take my car'?"

1. Chris said to Kathy, "The directions say, Make the second right onto Rock Road and then a quick left onto Williams Court."

2. Mrs. Bancroft said to her English literature class, "Tell me which famous writer said, To love oneself is the beginning of a lifelong romance."

3. Victoria said, "Crystal answered, Obviously, the writer who was in love with himself!"

4. Skye said, "Mrs. Bancroft replied, Perhaps that is true, but the answer is Oscar Wilde."

5. Then, Mrs. Bancroft said, "Now, tell me who said I have often regretted my speech, never my silence."

PRACTICE B Writing Quotations Within Quotations

Read the direct quotations below. Then, rewrite each quotation to be a quotation within a quotation.

Example: "The optimist proclaims that we live in the best of all possible worlds, and the pessimist fears this is true." —James Branch Cabell
Answer: Mrs. McBride told her class, "A wise man named James Branch Cabell once said, 'The optimist proclaims that we live in the best of all possible worlds, and the pessimist fears this is true.'"

1. "I am not young enough to know everything." —Oscar Wilde

   _____

2. "The covers of this book are too far apart." —Ambrose Bierce

   _____

3. "There are no facts, only interpretations." —Friedrich Nietzsche

   _____

4. "I find that the harder I work, the more luck I seem to have." —Thomas Jefferson

   _____

5. "Distrust any enterprise that requires new clothes." —Henry David Thoreau

   _____

Writing and Speaking Application

Write three quotations within quotations. Do not include single quotation marks. Exchange papers with a partner and add single quotation marks where they are needed in your partner's sentences. Then, read aloud your quotations.

116 PUNCTUATING EXPLANATORY MATERIAL WITHIN QUOTATIONS

Use square brackets ([ ]) to set off explanatory material within a direct quotation.

Sometimes, when a writer quotes a speaker directly, the writer adds explanatory information that was not part of the original quote. Such added information is bracketed to show that it was added.

Example: The principal said, "The new science labs [located in the west wing] have state-of-the-art equipment."

PRACTICE A Using Brackets for Explanatory Material Within Quotations

Read each item. Then, insert brackets where you think they are necessary.

Example: The vice principal said, "The construction of the new science labs which began in May took less time than anticipated."

Answer: The vice principal said, "The construction of the new science labs [which began in May] took less time than anticipated."

1. Mrs. Creighton said, "The play was written in 1614, two years before his William Shakespeare's death."

2. She explained, "Some critics Hodgkins and Fleming, among others questioned whether Shakespeare actually wrote the play."

3. Jane asked, "Why did they the critics think he didn't write the play?"

4. Mrs. Creighton answered, "Some theories suggest that Shakespeare did not write all the plays 39 he is credited with writing."

5. The mayor of Washington, D.C., is quoted as saying, "The city the District of Columbia is bankrupt. This is a crisis of great magnitude."

PRACTICE B Writing Quotations With Explanatory Material in Brackets

Read each item below. Then, write a direct quotation that includes the item as explanatory material in brackets.

Example: the United States and Canada

Answer: The president said, "The problem is one that our countries [the United States and Canada] share, and so we must share the solution as well."

1. until proven guilty _____

2. Houston, Texas _____

3. the incident _____

4. unwarranted _____

5. Red Cross workers _____

Writing and Speaking Application

Write five quotations with explanatory material. Do not include brackets. Exchange papers with a partner and add brackets where they are needed in your partner's quotations. Then, read aloud the quotations.

117 FORMATTING DIALOGUE

A conversation between two or more people is called **dialogue**. When writing dialogue, begin a new paragraph with each change of speaker. Use quotation marks to set off direct quotations. For quotations longer than a paragraph, put quotation marks at the beginning of each paragraph and at the end of the final paragraph. See the example below.

Example: At the school assembly, the principal announced, "We will no longer allow eleventh-graders to park in the west parking lot."

"Why not, Mr. Thompson?" asked the junior-class president.

PRACTICE A Using Quotation Marks and Paragraph Breaks in Dialogue

Read the dialogue below. Then, place quotation marks where they are needed, and add a slash (/) anywhere a new paragraph should begin.

Example: The principal announced, I will now take questions. A journalist from the school paper asked the principal, So, Mr. Thompson, how can you justify this new rule to the junior class?

Answer: The principal announced, "I will now take questions." / A journalist from the school paper asked the principal, "So, Mr. Thompson, how can you justify this new rule to the junior class?"

As I see it, the privileges that we have extended to the eleventh-graders have not been respected by them, answered Mr. Thompson. The journalist asked, What will you do with the extra spaces in the west parking lot? The principal replied, They will be offered to faculty and staff who before had to park on the street. The journalist asked, Mr. Thompson, what, if anything, can the junior class do to reverse your decision? The principal explained, As of now, I will not reverse my decision. Next year, when the eleventh-graders are seniors, they will enjoy the benefits of the new rule.

PRACTICE B Writing Dialogue With Quotation Marks and Paragraph Breaks

On the lines provided, write five lines of dialogue between a teenager interviewing for a job at a store and the store manager.

Example: Mrs. Fransessa asked, "What experience do you have?"

"I have been babysitting and helping at my parents' store for three years," Susan said.

_____

_____

_____

_____

_____

_____

_____

Writing and Speaking Application

Work with a partner to write three more lines for the dialogues you both wrote in Practice B. Be sure to use quotation marks and paragraph breaks correctly. Then, read the new dialogues aloud together.

118 USING QUOTATION MARKS FOR TITLES

Use quotation marks (" ") around the titles of most shorter works.

Quotation marks are used around titles of the following works: short stories, book chapters, short poems, essays, articles, written works that are part of a larger collection, television episodes or segments, podcast episodes or segments, songs, and parts of long musical compositions.

Example: The latest episode of my favorite television show is called "The Mouse Catcher."

PRACTICE A Placing Quotation Marks Around Titles

Read each sentence. Then, place quotation marks where they are needed.

Example: Please read The Love Song of J. Alfred Prufrock by T. S. Eliot for homework.
Answer: Please read "The Love Song of J. Alfred Prufrock" by T. S. Eliot for homework.

1. Sarah wrote a short story in creative writing class called The Near Miss.

2. Emma wrote a poem for the same class called Overcoming Me.

3. My favorite episode of this television show is called Rescue in the Sky.

4. I used an article titled How to End the War for my current events essay.

5. My teacher said that my essay Why the War Must End was one of the best he has ever read.

6. One of my favorite songs is Say What You Need to Say by John Mayer.

7. My uncle's favorite song of all time is Pinball Wizard by The Who.

8. I think one of the greatest poems ever written is The Road Not Taken by Robert Frost.

9. My English teacher prefers poems such as The Lantern Bearer by Robert Louis Stevenson.

10. The journalist finished his article The Fall of a President.

PRACTICE B Punctuating Titles in Sentences

For each item, write a sentence using the type of title indicated. Be sure to use quotation marks correctly in your sentence.

Example: essay title
Answer: I finally finished my essay, "John D. Rockefeller: Great Entrepreneur."

1. short story title _____

2. song title _____

3. short poem title _____

4. article title _____

5. television or podcast episode title _____

Writing and Speaking Application

Write three sentences including the titles of your choice. Do not include quotation marks. Exchange papers with a partner, and add quotation marks to the titles in each other's sentences. Then, take turns reading the new sentences and discuss placement of quotation marks.

119 USING UNDERLINING AND ITALICS

Underline or italicize the titles of full-length works; the names of ships and other vessels; foreign words; and words, letters, or numbers used as names for themselves.

Underlining and italics are used to make text stand out in writing. Use underlining in handwritten work; use italics in typed material. Underline or italicize the following: titles of books, newspapers, plays, long poems, magazines, movies, television and podcast series, long works of music, and works of art. Also underline or italicize the names of air-, sea-, and spacecraft; foreign words that have not yet been adopted into the English language; and words, letters, or numbers used as names for themselves.

Examples: My father reads the *Dallas Morning News* every day.
The *i*'s in her paper looked like numbers, not letters.
My grandmother said *buenas noches*, which means "good night," to me on the phone.

PRACTICE A Underlining (or Italicizing) Titles and Special Words

Read each sentence. Then, underline or italicize text as needed.

Example: Please read chapters 1 through 5 of Sula by Toni Morrison.
Answer: Please read chapters 1 through 5 of <u>Sula</u> by Toni Morrison.

1. I am writing a novel called Not in Kansas Anymore as my final project.

2. We saw the famous painting Mona Lisa in person.

3. I watch The Today Show every morning while I get ready for school.

4. Did you know that the Titanic sank on its maiden voyage?

5. My mother's favorite album is Revolver by The Beatles.

6. We are just starting to read Portrait in Sepia by Isabela Allende.

7. I hope it is as good as her other book, Daughter of Fortune.

8. When we went to Costa Rica, we said muchas gracias all the time.

9. My teacher took three points off my essay because I didn't cross my t's.

PRACTICE B Underlining (or Italicizing) Titles in Sentences

For each item, write a sentence using the type of title indicated. Be sure to underline or italicize the title correctly.

Example: newspaper title
Answer: I was considering getting a subscription to the <u>Wall Street Journal</u>.

1. book title _____

2. magazine title _____

3. play title _____

4. television or podcast series title _____

5. movie title _____

Writing and Speaking Application

Write three sentences with the titles of your choice. Do not underline the titles. Exchange papers with a partner, and underline the titles in each other's sentences. Then, take turns reading the new sentences, and discuss what you underlined.

120 USING QUOTATION MARKS TO INDICATE SARCASM AND IRONY

Use quotation marks (" ") to set off words intended as sarcasm or irony.

Example: My "kind and thoughtful" brother stranded me at the movie theater to go hang out with his friends.

PRACTICE A Adding Quotation Marks to Indicate Sarcasm or Irony

Read each sentence. Then, add quotation marks to indicate sarcasm or irony.

Example: Hey, Slugger, are you going to strike out yet again?
Answer: Hey, "Slugger," are you going to strike out yet again?

1. Are you going to invite Miss Personality to the party?
2. Your so-called jokes don't bother me a bit.
3. Whenever we go out, Luis conveniently forgets his wallet.
4. When I failed my driving test, my brother called me Mario Andretti all day.
5. When the car broke down for the second time, my mother exclaimed she was so happy my father had fixed it.
6. Whenever we are talking in class too much, our teacher thanks us for being so quiet.
7. We went to the supposed Sunshine State for vacation, and it rained the entire time.
8. We stopped at a restaurant in Wisconsin, the alleged Cheese State, and the waitress said they were out of cheeseburgers.
9. Today's special at the school cafeteria was mystery meat and petrified potatoes.
10. When I told my father I couldn't fix the lawnmower, he said it isn't exactly rocket science.

PRACTICE B Writing and Punctuating Sarcasm or Irony

For each item, write a sentence using the expression provided, along with quotation marks to indicate sarcasm or irony.

Example: best friend
Answer: I found out today that my "best friend" was talking behind my back!

1. joke _____
2. ray of sunshine _____
3. a real winner _____
4. rocket scientist _____
5. Brother of the Year award _____

Writing and Speaking Application

Work with a partner. Write four sentences that express irony or sarcasm. Do not use quotation marks. Exchange papers with your partner, and insert quotation marks where you think they are needed. Then, read aloud the sentences, and discuss the irony or sarcasm.

Name _____ Date _____

121 USING HYPHENS WITH NUMBERS

Use a hyphen (-) to write a compound number, a fraction used as an adjective, or any other numerical compound used as an adjective.

See the examples below.

Use a hyphen to write out a two-word number from twenty-one to ninety-nine.	My grandfather turned eighty-one years old yesterday.
Use a hyphen when a fraction is used as an adjective.	I used one-third cup of sour cream.
Use a hyphen when a number and a noun form a compound adjective.	We took a sixty-minute bike ride.
When two or more numbers modify the same word, use a hyphen after each number.	The eleventh- and twelfth-grade students gathered in the cafeteria.

PRACTICE A Hyphenating Numbers

Read each item. Then, add a hyphen or hyphens as needed.

Example: two thirds cup of soup
Answer: two-thirds cup of soup

1. ninety nine students
2. thirty six inches
3. twenty one miles
4. one-half box of pasta
5. two thirds cup of marinara sauce

6. the ninth and tenth grade students
7. a five minute break
8. a two minute phone call
9. a one hour run
10. twenty two years old

PRACTICE B Writing With Hyphenated Numbers

For each item, write a sentence using the numerical item indicated. Be sure to hyphenate correctly.

Example: sixty eight inches
Answer: The nurse told me that I was sixty-eight inches tall.

1. one third cup

_____

2. twenty one

_____

3. eighty six

_____

4. five mile run

_____

5. fifth and sixth period classes

_____

Writing and Speaking Application

Write three sentences with compound numbers and fractions. Do not hyphenate them. Exchange papers with a partner, and hyphenate the compound numbers and fractions in each other's sentences. Then, take turns reading the new sentences, and discuss what you hyphenated.

122 USING HYPHENS WITH PREFIXES AND SUFFIXES

Use a hyphen (-) to connect certain prefixes and suffixes to a base word.

Most prefixes and suffixes do not require a hyphen. By convention, however, a hyphen is used to connect the prefix *all-*, *ex-*, or *self-* or the suffix *-elect* to a base word. A hyphen is also used to connect any prefix to a proper noun or a proper adjective. See the examples below.

EXAMPLES: post-Shakespeare
self-confidence
president-elect

PRACTICE A Using Hyphens With Prefixes and Suffixes

Read the items below. Then, hyphenate them as needed.

Example: pro Americanism
Answer: pro-Americanism

1. self esteem
2. all state
3. mid March
4. pre Victorian
5. pro Democrat

6. post Easter
7. governor elect
8. mid June
9. ex boyfriend
10. all powerful

PRACTICE B Writing With Hyphenated Prefixes and Suffixes

Read each item. Then, write a sentence using the item and a hyphen.

Example: ex girlfriend
Answer: Juan ran into his ex-girlfriend at the mall, and they spoke briefly.

1. self taught _____

2. all encompassing _____

3. mid February _____

4. self motivation _____

5. ex Marine _____

6. pro British _____

7. ex husband _____

8. mayor elect _____

9. all out _____

10. self contained _____

Writing and Speaking Application

Work with a partner. Use a dictionary to find five examples of hyphenated words with suffixes and prefixes. Use each word you found in a sentence. Then, take turns reading aloud the new sentences.

123 USING HYPHENS WITH COMPOUND WORDS

Use a hyphen (-) to write certain compound nouns and to write a compound adjective that precedes the word it modifies.

Some compound nouns are hyphenated by convention. Use a dictionary to check whether a compound noun should be hyphenated.

Use a hyphen to connect the parts of a compound adjective that comes before the noun it modifies. The exceptions to this rule include adverbs ending in *-ly* and compound proper adjectives or compound proper nouns that are acting as an adjective. When compound modifiers follow a noun, they generally do not require the use of a hyphen. See the examples below.

Use Hyphens	Do Not Use Hyphens
ten-year-old girl well-made pair of jeans	widely available information The jeans were well made.

PRACTICE A Using Hyphens in Compound Nouns and Adjectives

Read each item. Then, add a hyphen or hyphens as needed. If you are unsure whether a compound noun should be hyphenated, check a dictionary.

Example: hard and fast rule
Answer: hard-and-fast rule

1. well to do gentleman
2. brother in law
3. bleary eyed child
4. above water rescue
5. sister in law

6. thirty year old man
7. in season produce
8. merry go round
9. up to date information
10. fifty year old woman

PRACTICE B Writing With Compound Nouns and Adjectives

Read each item. Then, write a sentence using the item and hyphens as needed. If you are unsure whether a compound noun should be hyphenated, check a dictionary.

Example: jack of all trades
Answer: My uncle who has worked as a carpenter, an electrician, and a plumber is known as a jack-of-all-trades.

1. court martial _____
2. take off _____
3. go between _____
4. friendly looking _____
5. easy going _____
6. sixteen year old _____
7. off season _____
8. well known _____
9. mass produced _____
10. as is _____

Writing and Speaking Application

Work with a partner. Use a dictionary to find five examples of hyphenated compound words. Use each word in a sentence. Then, take turns reading aloud the new sentences.

124 USING HYPHENS FOR CLARITY

Use a hyphen (-) to connect a prefix or a suffix to a base word when doing so will improve readability.

Some words with prefixes or suffixes can be misread if a hyphen is not used. Use a hyphen to connect a prefix or a suffix to a base word when a combination of letters might otherwise be confusing. The prefixes *semi-*, *anti-*, *de-*, *re-*, *pre-*, and *co-* are usually hyphenated when the prefix ends with the same letter that the base word begins with. Similarly, the suffixes *-less* and *-like* are usually hyphenated when the base word ends with the letters *ll*.

Example: We live in a **co-op** building, which means my parents own a share of the entire building.

PRACTICE A Adding Hyphens for Clarity
Read the items below. Then, hyphenate the words as needed.

Example: reencounter
Answer: re-encounter

1. semiinformative _____
2. reestablish _____
3. skillless _____
4. semiillustrative _____
5. deemphasize _____

6. reenlist _____
7. antiinflammatory _____
8. reenergize _____
9. semiindependent _____
10. antiindependence _____

PRACTICE B Using Hyphens for Clarity in Sentences
Read the sentences below. Then, rewrite each sentence, correcting errors in hyphenation. If the punctuation is correct, write correct.

Example: After moving 3,000 miles away five years ago, Chris suddenly called me to reestablish our friendship.

Answer: After moving 3,000 miles away five years ago, Chris suddenly called me to re-establish our friendship.

1. The brisk walk reenergized us to go back and study more for our final exam.

_____

2. The gown had a belllike silhouette, flaring below the knees.

_____

3. The semiinclusive parking lot at our school is for seniors and faculty only.

_____

4. Pet squabbles at work have been threatening my pre-existing friendship with Kai.

_____

5. A group of demonstrators were antiimperialistic and wanted their independence.

_____

Writing and Speaking Application
Work with a partner. Use a dictionary to find five examples of words that are hyphenated for clarity. Use each word you found in a sentence, but omit the hyphen. Then, exchange papers with your partner, and add hyphens as needed. Take turns reading aloud the sentences, and discuss the use of hyphens.

Name _____ Date _____

125 USING HYPHENS AT THE ENDS OF LINES

Use a hyphen (-) to divide a word at the end of a line of text.

Sometimes, a long word at the end of a line of text is hyphenated, with part of the word appearing on the next line. This keeps the line length even, making the text easier to read.

When you use a computer or another electronic device to write, the software will usually add these hyphens automatically. When you handwrite, however, you may need to add hyphens yourself.

If a word must be divided, always divide it between syllables, and always place the hyphen at the end of the first line, not at the beginning of the second line. Do not hyphenate one-syllable words.

Example: The junior class president will provide information about the fundraiser tomorrow morning.

PRACTICE A Using Hyphens to Correctly Divide Words

Read each word. Then, rewrite it as if it had to be hyphenated. Put the hyphen in the correct place. If you are unsure where one syllable ends and the next begins, check a dictionary.

Example: support
Answer: sup-port

1. classroom _____
2. notebook _____
3. overheard _____
4. diving _____
5. ticket _____

6. sleeping _____
7. surgeon _____
8. focus _____
9. guiding _____
10. textbook _____

PRACTICE B Using Hyphens Correctly at the End of Lines

Read each sentence. Then, rewrite the incorrectly divided word, showing how it should be divided, if at all. Remember that one-syllable words should not be divided.

Example: The principal walked around the school looking for the student who lost his keys.
Answer: look-ing

1. I forgot to bring my wallet to the mall, so I could not buy anything for my mother's birthday.

_____

2. The football players ran onto the field and warmed up before the game.

_____

3. Everyone at the senior class meeting was talking at once, so the vice principal told us to be quiet.

_____

4. The fans applauded for the basketball players as they ran onto the court.

_____

Writing and Speaking Application

Write three sentences in which a word breaks to the next line. Switch papers with a partner. If a word has been incorrectly divided, then correct the error. Then, read aloud and discuss the sentences.

126 USING HYPHENS CORRECTLY TO DIVIDE WORDS

When using hyphens to divide words, keep the following rules in mind.

Do not divide one-syllable words.	Incorrect: jud-ge Correct: judge
Do not divide a word so that a single letter or the letters *ed* stand alone.	Incorrect: read-y Correct: ready
Avoid dividing proper nouns and proper adjectives.	Incorrect: Ameri-can Correct: American
Do not further divide a word that is already hyphenated.	We are going to visit my brother and my sister-in-law in Toronto.

PRACTICE A Using Hyphens Correctly to Divide Words

Read each divided word. If the word is hyphenated correctly, write correct. *If the word is hyphenated incorrectly, write the word the way it should appear.*

Example: wish-ed
Answer: wished

1. cloth-ed _____
2. day-light _____
3. thor-ough _____
4. to-day _____
5. lod-ge _____

6. Aman-da _____
7. run-ning _____
8. qui-et _____
9. Brit-ish _____
10. stead-y _____

PRACTICE B Rewriting Incorrectly Divided Words

Read each group of divided words. Identify the word that is not correctly divided. Then, rewrite the word, putting the hyphen in the correct place, or writing it as one word if it cannot be divided.

Example: warm-ed   warm-ing   warm-er
Answer: warmed

1. cloth-es   cloth-ing   wash-cloth _____
2. fan-ned   farm-er   frank-ness _____
3. flavor-ful   fo-ol   fruit-less _____
4. base-ball   bor-ed   broom-stick _____
5. bl-ack   guilt-less   grate-ful _____
6. spell-ed   for-lorn   crim-son _____
7. tele-graph   sing-along   te-ll _____
8. finall-y   fam-ished   fam-ous _____

Writing and Speaking Application

Write three pairs of words. For each pair, include one word that is divided correctly and one that is divided incorrectly. Exchange papers with a partner, and identify the incorrect word in each pair. Then, provide the corrections, and discuss them with your partner.

Name _____ Date _____

127 USING APOSTROPHES TO FORM POSSESSIVE NOUNS

Use an apostrophe (') to create the possessive form of a noun.

Apostrophes are used with nouns to show ownership or possession. See the rules for possessive nouns and the examples below.

Add an apostrophe and -s to create the possessive form of most singular nouns.	the student's lunch the bird's nest
Add only an apostrophe to create the possessive form of plural nouns ending in -s or -es.	five birds' nests the knives' handles
Add an apostrophe and an -s to create the possessive form of plural nouns that do not end in -s or -es.	the children's games two deer's tracks
Add an apostrophe and -s (or just an apostrophe if the word is a plural ending in -s) to the last word of a compound noun.	my brother-in-law's golf clubs
Use an apostrophe and -s (or just an apostrophe if the word is a plural ending in -s) to form possessives involving time, amount, or the word *sake*.	a day's rest three cents' worth for Chris's sake

PRACTICE A Using Apostrophes to Form Possessive Nouns

Read each item below. Then, write the possessive form of the noun in parentheses. Be sure to place the apostrophe correctly.

Example: the (players) best game
Answer: player's

1. my (family) home _____
2. the (girls) backpacks _____
3. the (foxes) den _____
4. the (skaters) awards _____
5. the (Smiths) cars _____
6. the (mice) squeaks _____
7. my (sister-in-law) brother _____
8. the (gentlemen) scarves _____

PRACTICE B Using Apostrophes Correctly in Sentences

Read each sentence. Then, rewrite the sentence, correcting any mistakes with possessive nouns.

Example: The athletes medal is gold.
Answer: The athlete's medal is gold.

1. Mr. Fine does not approve of his sons wives. _____

2. Having four students with the same name in her class added to the new teachers confusion.

3. Mary Garcias goal was to write a best-selling novel.

4. Mrs. Gonzalez' grandchildren gave her a surprise birthday dinner.

5. The disaster was averted and hundreds of lives saved due to Nilss quick thinking.

Writing and Speaking Application

Work with a partner. Write five sentences using possessive nouns. Do not include apostrophes. Exchange papers, and add apostrophes as needed. Then, take turns reading aloud the sentences, and discuss the placement of apostrophes.

128 USING APOSTROPHES WITH PRONOUNS

Use an apostrophe (') to create the possessive form of an indefinite pronoun.

Apostrophes are used with some pronouns to show ownership or possession, but not with others. See the rules for possessive pronouns and the examples below.

Use an apostrophe and *-s* to create the possessive form of an indefinite pronoun.	somebody's car each other's feelings
Do **not** use an apostrophe with possessive personal pronouns; their form already shows ownership.	This hockey stick is hers. The backpack hanging on the hook is his. The best idea I heard was theirs.
Be careful not to confuse the contractions *who's, it's,* and *they're* with possessive pronouns.	Whose sweater is this? (Whose = possessive pronoun) Who's going shopping today? (Whose = Who is)

PRACTICE A Forming Possessive Pronouns

Read each item. Then, write the correct possessive form of the pronoun. If the item is correct, write correct.

Example: whose address
Answer: <u>correct</u>

1. someones phone _____
2. somebodies baseball glove _____
3. this essay of his _____
4. anybodys guess _____
5. neithers idea _____

6. ones feelings _____
7. no ones car _____
8. that application of her's _____
9. somebodys tennis racket _____
10. anyones help _____

PRACTICE B Using Apostrophes Correctly With Indefinite Pronouns

Read each indefinite pronoun below. Then, write a sentence of your own using the possessive form of the indefinite pronoun.

Example: someone
Answer: <u>Someone's wallet is on the floor.</u>

1. everybody _____
2. everyone _____
3. neither _____
4. either _____
5. one _____
6. anybody _____
7. someone _____
8. somebody _____

Writing and Speaking Application

Work with a partner. Write five sentences using possessive pronouns. Do not include apostrophes. Exchange papers, and add apostrophes as needed. Then, take turns reading aloud the sentences, and discuss the placement of apostrophes.

Name _____ Date _____

129 USING APOSTROPHES TO FORM CONTRACTIONS

Use an apostrophe (') to replace the letter or letters omitted in a contraction.

A **contraction** is a shortening of two (or more) words so that they are written and pronounced as a single word. Contractions are commonly used in informal speech and writing. An apostrophe is used in a contraction in place of the letter or letters that have been omitted from the original words. Here are some common types of contractions:

- a form of the verb *be* plus the adverb *not*
  Examples: *was not = wasn't; is not = isn't; are not = aren't*
- a helping verb (such as *do, have, will,* or *can*) plus the adverb *not*
  Examples: *does not = doesn't; had not = hadn't; will not = won't* (underline)irregular(/underline); *cannot = can't*
- a pronoun plus a form of the verb *be*
  Examples: *I am = I'm; you are = you're; she is = she's; it is = it's*
- a pronoun plus a helping verb (such as *have, will,* or *would*)
  Examples: *I have = I've; you will = you'll; they would = they'd*

PRACTICE A Using Apostrophes to Form Contractions

Read each item. Then, combine the words into a contraction. Be sure to include an apostrophe in the correct location.

Example: should not
Answer: shouldn't

1. are not _____
2. will not _____
3. he will _____
4. I am _____
5. she will _____

6. I would _____
7. we have _____
8. you are _____
9. she is _____
10. they are _____

PRACTICE B Using Apostrophes Correctly in Contractions

Read the words below. Then, write a sentence of your own using a contraction in place of the words. Be sure to include an apostrophe in the correct location.

Example: we are
Answer: We're sitting at the same table at the junior prom.

1. are not _____
2. she has _____
3. should not _____
4. will not _____
5. I have _____
6. they are _____
7. we are _____
8. he would _____

Writing and Speaking Application

Write a brief paragraph about your weekend plans. Do not include contractions or apostrophes. Underline the words that can be made into contractions. Exchange papers with a partner, and add the contractions with apostrophes where indicated. Then, take turns reading aloud the rewritten paragraphs, and discuss the placement of contractions.

130 USING APOSTROPHES TO CREATE SPECIAL PLURALS

Use an apostrophe (') and -s to create the plural form of a numeral, a symbol, a letter, or a word used as a name for itself.

Apostrophes can help avoid confusion with special plurals. See the example below.

Example: I received four *A*'s and two *B*'s on my report card.

PRACTICE A Using Apostrophes to Create Special Plurals

Read the items below. Then, rewrite the items, inserting apostrophes to create special plurals.

Example: ps and qs
Answer: p's and q's

1. nos _____
2. Cs and Ds _____
3. ifs, ands, or buts _____
4. Is _____
5. 3s and 4s _____

6. ABCs _____
7. 123s _____
8. +s and −s _____
9. ?s _____
10. !s _____

PRACTICE B Using Apostrophes to Create Special Plurals in Sentences

Read the items below. Use each item in a sentence, including apostrophes to avoid confusion.

Example: !s
Answer: There are too many !'s in your personal narrative.

1. ABC _____
2. As and Bs _____
3. 5s _____
4. As and Ans _____
5. Is and yous _____
6. ?s _____
7. :s and ;s _____
8. 10s and 20s _____
9. ps and qs _____
10. Fs _____

Writing and Speaking Application

Work with a partner. Write five sentences that contain plurals of letters, numbers, words, and symbols. Do not include apostrophes. Exchange papers with your partner, and add the apostrophes as needed. Then, take turns reading the sentences aloud, and discuss the placement of apostrophes.

131 USING PARENTHESES

Use parentheses, ( ), to enclose an explanation or other information that may be omitted from the rest of a sentence without changing its basic meaning or construction.

If the information in the parentheses is a phrase, do not use an initial capital letter or an end punctuation mark inside the parentheses. If the material in the parentheses is a complete sentence, use an initial capital letter, and place an end mark inside the parentheses. Use parentheses to set off a numerical explanation, such as the years of a person's birth and death or the year(s) during which an event occurred.

Examples: We went to Corpus Christi (in the southeastern part of the state) to visit my uncle.

New Hampshire is known for its mountains and maple trees. (See the photos below for examples.)

Orson Welles (1915–1985) wrote, directed, and starred in the film *Citizen Kane*.

PRACTICE A Revising to Add Parenthetical Information to Sentences

Read each sentence. Then, rewrite each sentence, adding the items indicated in parentheses where appropriate in the sentence. If the item is correct as it appears, write correct.

Example: Flannery O'Connor was a Southern Gothic writer. (1925–1964)
Answer: Flannery O'Connor (1925–1964) was a Southern Gothic writer.

1. The poet Emily Dickinson spent most of her life in Amherst. (a medium-sized town in Massachusetts)

   _____

2. In August of A.D. 79, there were signs that the volcano Vesuvius was again about to erupt. (in southwestern Italy) _____

3. Fruit flies are often used as model organisms in genetic research. (scientific name *Drosophila melanogaster*) _____

4. Thomas Jefferson served two terms as president of the United States. (1801–1809)

   _____

PRACTICE B Writing Sentences With Parenthetical Information

Read the items below. Use each item in parentheses in a sentence of your own.

Example: (chemistry and algebra)
Answer: I have to take exams in two classes tomorrow (chemistry and algebra), so I need to get a good night's rest.

1. (college applications) _____

2. (school year 2022–2023) _____

3. (in Fort Worth, Texas) _____

4. (the prom committee) _____

5. (I had written the wrong assignment in my agenda.) _____

Writing and Speaking Application

Write five sentences that contain parenthetical material, such as dates or any other nonessential information. Do not include the parentheses. Exchange papers with a partner, and add the parentheses as needed. Then, read aloud and discuss the sentences.

132 USING BRACKETS

Use square brackets, [ ], to enclose an explanatory word or phrase added to the words of another writer or speaker.

Use brackets to enclose words you insert in quotations when quoting someone else. Note that the Latin expression *sic* (meaning "thus") is sometimes enclosed in brackets to show that the author of the quoted material has made an error, such as a misspelling, in a word or phrase.

Example: "A universal languge [*sic*] could be monitored, the pronunciation kept constant, the script guarded from local [or nationalistic] peculiarities."

PRACTICE A Using Brackets in Quotations

Read each quotation. Then, rewrite it, adding the bracketed item where you think it is appropriate.

Example: "The air in the cave was stail and smelled unpleasant." [*sic*]
Answer: "The air in the cave was stail [sic] and smelled unpleasant."

1. "The light from our miner's lamps penetrated the darkness, and we could see only where the light fell, so we had to feel our way among the rocks." [barely] _____

_____

2. "Often, we slipped down inclines or fell into potholes and pools." [very steep]

_____

3. "Even though we moved, we soon became wet and bruised." [cautiously]

_____

4. "Finally, we crawled through a low place." [very] _____

_____

5. "We came out into a big space with a poole." [*sic*] _____

_____

PRACTICE B Revising to Add Brackets to Quotations

Read each quotation. Then, rewrite it, adding sic *in brackets where needed.*

Example: "We walked towards the ralings, which proved to contain a gate."
Answer: "We walked towards the ralings [sic], which proved to contain a gate."

1. "Ian Young opened it with a click of iron, and it swung on unoyled hinges."

_____

2. "Beyond it, the dim light showed the forelorn public garden."

_____

3. "Their were a few seats beside the path."

_____

4. "But in late November, the melancoly of such places could seep into the soul like fungus."

_____

5. "Ian Young walked purposefuly onward, neither hurrying nor moving with caution."

_____

Writing and Speaking Application

Work with a partner. Write five sentences that contain material that should be bracketed. Do not include the brackets. Exchange papers with your partner, and add the brackets where you think they belong. Then, take turns reading the sentences aloud, and discuss the placement of the brackets.

133 USING ELLIPSES

Use an ellipsis (. . .) to show an omission in a direct quotation or a pause or an interruption in dialogue. The plural of *ellipsis* is *ellipses*.

An ellipsis shows where a word or words have been omitted from a quoted passage. It can also mark a pause or interruption in dialogue. See the examples below.

Use an ellipsis to show that a word or words have been omitted from a quotation.	**Original:** According to the author, "Nearly 2,000 residents out of a population of 5,800 contracted the virus." **With Ellipsis:** According to the author, "Nearly 2,000 residents . . . contracted the virus."
Use an ellipsis to mark a pause or an interruption in speech or dialogue.	I said to the children, "OK, kids, ready . . . set . . . go!"

PRACTICE A Using Ellipses to Show Omissions in Quotations

Read each quotation. Then, rewrite it, using an ellipsis to show the omission of the words in parentheses.

Example: "Our country was invaded in 1941, and almost immediately my sister and I enlisted in the Armed Forces." (almost immediately)

Answer: "Our country was invaded in 1941, and . . . my sister and I enlisted in the Armed Forces."

1. "Umbrellas are seldom useful in Chicago because of the city's strong winds." (city's)
   _____

2. "Prying up the disguised trap door, we discovered a secret chamber, once a station on the Underground Railroad." (a secret chamber, once) _____

3. "My friend Jarmila knows I love to cook, so she brought me a cookbook full of recipes." (knows I love to cook, so she) _____

4. "Mary Stewart wrote the novel *Airs Above the Ground*." (the novel) _____
   _____

5. "Of the three Watson girls, only Rhonda called me." (Watson) _____
   _____

PRACTICE B Using Ellipses to Show Pauses in Dialogue

Read each line of dialogue. Then, rewrite the line, adding one or more ellipses to show pauses where it makes sense for the speaker to have paused.

Example: "I really don't know how or if I'll ever finish these applications."
Answer: "I really don't know how . . . or if . . . I'll ever finish these applications."

1. "If these walls could talk I wonder what they'd say." _____
2. "Mom, Vincent had a car accident but he isn't hurt." _____
3. "Oh, thank goodness what happened?" _____
4. "I don't know where to start; it all happened so fast!" _____
5. "This is why I worry so much about the two of you." _____

Writing and Speaking Application

Work with a partner. Write six sentences that contain material that can be omitted. Do not include the ellipses. Exchange papers with your partner, and replace the words you think can be omitted with ellipses. Then, take turns reading the new sentences aloud, and discuss the placement of the ellipses.

Name _____ Date _____

134 USING DASHES

Use a dash (—) or dashes to signal a strong interruption or pause.

Dashes signal stronger, more sudden interruptions in thought or speech than commas or parentheses. A dash may also take the place of certain words before an explanation. See the examples below.

Use a dash or dashes to indicate an abrupt change of thought, a dramatic interrupting idea, or a summary statement.	You actually believed her—I told you never to believe a word she says—when she told you she went skydiving!
Use a dash or dashes to set off a nonessential appositive or modifier when it is long, already punctuated, or especially dramatic.	The car salesman—tired of helping the impossible customer—simply walked out of the showroom.
Use a dash or dashes to set off a parenthetical expression when it is long, already punctuated, or especially dramatic.	We visited the Vietnam Veterans Memorial—what an experience!—on our trip to Washington, D.C.

PRACTICE A Using Dashes to Emphasize Parenthetical Expressions

Read each sentence. Then, rewrite it, using dashes to emphasize the parenthetical expression.

Example: After a four-hour flight what a long trip! we finally arrived at our vacation destination.
Answer: After a four-hour flight—what a long trip!—we finally arrived at our vacation destination.

1. The flight I have never seen such a crowded airplane was delayed for three hours. _____
_____

2. What was the cause I hate when planes are late for the delay? _____
_____

3. We don't know the reason we think it was mechanical because the pilot never told us. _____
_____

4. What did you do I never know what to do on a crowded airplane while you waited? _____
_____

5. I read my book it is the best book ever the entire time. _____
_____

PRACTICE B Using Dashes for Emphasis in Sentences

Read each expression below. Then, write a sentence of your own, using the parenthetical expression provided and dashes for emphasis.

Example: what a surprise!
Answer: My friends threw me a birthday party—what a surprise!—two days before the actual day.

1. I can't believe I won! _____

2. I was so disappointed! _____

3. my father was furious! _____

4. what a close game _____

5. can you imagine? _____

Writing and Speaking Application

Work with a partner. Write five sentences that contain parenthetical expressions. Do not set them off with dashes. Exchange papers with your partner, and add the dashes for emphasis. Then, take turns reading the sentences aloud, and discuss the placement of the dashes.

135 USING SLASHES

A slash is used to separate numbers in dates and fractions, lines of quoted poetry, or options. Slashes are also used to separate parts of an Internet address.

Use slashes to separate the month, day, and year in dates and to separate the numerator and denominator in fractions. Slashes are also used to indicate line breaks in up to three lines of quoted poetry in continuous text. (When quoting poetry, insert a space on either side of the slash.) Slashes can separate choices or options, representing the words *and* and *or*. Finally, slashes are used to separate the various parts of an Internet address, or URL.

Date	3/14/2018 (March 14, 2018)
Fraction	2/3 cup of milk
Line of Quoted Poetry	I used these lines from a Walt Whitman poem: "Oh Captain! my Captain! our fearful trip is done, / The ship has weather'd every rack, the prize we / sought is won."
Options	Please choose one: oatmeal / eggs / toast.
Internet Address (URL)	http://www.whitehouse.gov/ (the White House)

PRACTICE A Using Slashes With Numbers

Read each item. Then, rewrite it, using numerals and a slash or slashes.

Example: July 8, 1995
Answer: 7/8/1995

1. three-tenths _____
2. one-fifth _____
3. January 22, 2012 _____
4. May 11, 2023 _____
5. March 3, 1996 _____

6. six-elevenths _____
7. one-third _____
8. November 28, 1968 _____
9. December 11, 2017 _____
10. one-twentieth _____

PRACTICE B Using Slashes Correctly in Sentences

Read each sentence below. Then, add slashes where needed.

Example: The community pool party was held on 6 24 2022.
Answer: The community pool party was held on 6/24/2022.

1. Choose one of these options: spring rolls soup salad chicken skewers.

2. The local elections that year were held on 10 2 2020.

3. My eldest cousin was born on 4 7 1999.

4. The options for lunch today are as follows: grilled fish grilled chicken grilled cheese.

5. The state standardized test was scheduled to be held on 1 19 2022.

Writing and Speaking Application

Work with a partner. Write five sentences that contain dates, fractions, and options. Do not include slashes. Exchange papers with your partner, and add the slashes as needed. Then, take turns reading the sentences aloud, and discuss the placement of the slashes.